"**If** you don't have anything nice to say...

come sit next to me"

"If you don't have anything nice to say...

come sit next to me"

Coral Amende

Macmillan • USA

MACMILLAN
A Prentice Hall Macmillan Company
15 Columbus Circle
New York, NY 10023

Library of Congress Cataloging-in-Publication Data
If you don't have anything nice to say . . . come sit next to me
   [compiled by] Coral Amende.
       p. cm.
     Includes index.
     ISBN 0-02-860043-6
     1. Celebrities--Quotations, maxims, etc. I. Amende, Coral.
II. Title: If you don't have anything nice to say . . . come sit next to me.
PN6084.C44I38   1995
792--dc20   94-36619
                                                      CIP

Designed by Carla Weise/Levavi & Levavi

Manufactured in the United States of America
10 9 8 7 6 5 4 3 2 1

Many thanks to Jim DiGiovanni, Mary Ann Lynch,
Deirdre Mullane, Argo-May Rosner, and Laura Wood.

Contents

Foreword

Today's gossip is tomorrow's headline.

WALTER WINCHELL

Human beings have an undeniable fascination with gossip. It may be one of our baser instincts, but as tattle queen Barbara Walters says, "Show me someone who never gossips and I'll show you someone who isn't interested in people." When those people are famous, it becomes even more interesting—and delicious.

Michael Musto, gossip columnist for New York City's *Village Voice*, writes that "star behavior is more compelling than yours (or even mine), and the day the Oscar nominations are announced surpasses any political election results in impact, however perverse that sense of priorities might seem." But in defense of this seemingly prurient interest, he rationalizes that "anyone who admits to being completely satisfied with the excitement and romance of his own existence is at an unfair advantage because he probably enjoys the added bonus of being a liar."

Musto's right. Whatever personal reasons we may have, we all love to "dish the dirt," whether it's about friends and co-workers or our most revered public figures. And it does serve a purpose: At its most rudimentary level, gossip is an informal social chronicle of a particular time, characterizing more accurately than history books the personalities who themselves help shape and define an era.

Well-aimed barbs have started some of the world's great love affairs, and even greater feuds (see Joan Crawford on Bette Davis and vice-versa, for one good example). Hero status doesn't guarantee immunity—not by a long shot. Even our most venerated icons aren't safe from the wickedly sharp tongues of self-proclaimed critics like Gene Simmons, leader of the rock band KISS, who has no great respect for Shakespeare (the bad boy bad-mouths the Bard on page 138; we can only speculate as to what Shakespeare's opinion of KISS would have been!). And sometimes quotes say as much about the speaker as they do the subject (see Charles Manson on Adolf Hitler, Jessica Tandy on Hume Cronyn, and Madonna on Sandra Bernhard).

Yes, the gossipy gang's all here—pop stars and politicos, authors and *hauteurs*, soldiers and socialites, band leaders and boxers. From the waggish to the wise, the profound to the profane, the subversive to the sublime, you'll read in the pages ahead a few of the good and lots of the bad and downright ugly things the famous have said about one another. Enjoy!

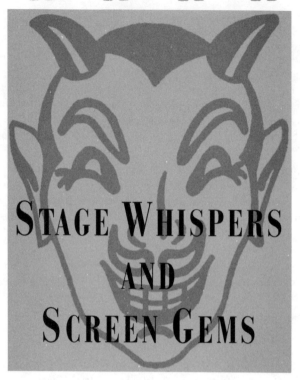

CHAPTER ONE

STAGE WHISPERS
AND
SCREEN GEMS

"An actor is a guy who, if you ain't talking about
him, ain't listening."

MARLON BRANDO

WOODY ALLEN   FILM DIRECTOR, ACTOR

Woody is at two with nature.   **Dick Cavett**

There's no question that the Woody Allen character that appears
on the screen is a Greek god version of what he's like in real life. I
met him once and he tried to hide behind Mia Farrow.

John Cleese

I went up to Woody Allen, "Oh, Mr. Allen, I really admire your
work. I think you're terrific. And I read somewhere that you're
very shy, so I feel we've something in common. I'm shy too." He
just looked at me and said, "Well, you could've fooled me."

Joan Collins

He could have been a fashion designer. He's interested in
women's clothes.   **Mia Farrow**

I can't make head or tail out of half of what he says.

Diane Keaton

Before we shot that kissing scene in *The Front* Woody Allen said,
"I'm going to give you only one lip when we kiss. Because if I give
you two you'll never live through it."   **Andrea Marcovicci**

PEDRO ALMODÓVAR   FILM DIRECTOR

Like him? We're getting married!   **John Waters**

JULIE ANDREWS   SINGER, ACTRESS

Before I'd met Julie, some people were conjecturing about her
success. I said, "I can tell you what that is. She has lilacs for
pubic hair."   **Blake Edwards**

Julie Andrews is like a nun with a switchblade.   **Leslie Halliwell**

Working with her is like being hit over the head with a
Valentine's card.   **Christopher Plummer**

HAL ASHBY FILM DIRECTOR, *SHAMPOO*

You have more respect for a bad film from Fritz Lang than for a good film from Hal Ashby—if there were any good films from Hal Ashby, which there are not.   **Jean-Luc Godard**

FRED ASTAIRE DEBONAIR ACTOR, DANCER, CHOREOGRAPHER

No dancer can watch Fred Astaire and not know that we all should have been in another business.   **Mikhail Baryshnikov**

Fred Astaire danced himself so thin I could almost spit through him.   **Bing Crosby**

He is the nearest we are ever likely to get to a human Mickey Mouse.   **Graham Greene**

DAN AYKROYD COMEDIAN, ACTOR

I don't think Dan Aykroyd would be as funny if he were built like a marathon runner. I find it refreshing that people like Dan let their bodies go to seed.   **Liam Neeson**

CARROLL BAKER ACTRESS, *BABY DOLL*

More bomb than bombshell.   **Judith Crist**

ALEC BALDWIN ACTOR

He's gorgeous. I saw him at a restaurant, and I was salivating at the mouth. He has a potbelly, but I could get over that.   **Rosie Perez**

ANNE BANCROFT ACTRESS

... may be the only leading lady today with the ability to cross one eye without moving the other.   **Vincent Canby**

TALLULAH BANKHEAD ACTRESS

A parrot around Tallulah must feel as frustrated as a kleptomaniac in a piano store.   **Fred Allen**

Don't look now, Tallulah, but your show's slipping.

Heywood Broun

Queen of the Nil.   **John Mason Brown**

A day away from Tallulah is like a month in the country.

Howard Dietz

Miss Bankhead will never again act in a play of mine because I can only stand a certain amount of boredom.   **Lillian Hellman**

I've staged shows that called for the management of a herd of buffalo and I've shot actors out of cannons for fifty feet into the arms of an adagio dancer, but both of them were easier than saying good morning to Miss Bankhead.   **Billy Rose**

Early in my career I was in my dressing room making up. Suddenly I turned around and there was this totally naked woman. "What's the matter, dahling?" Tallulah Bankhead said. "Haven't you ever seen a blonde before?"   **Donald Sutherland**

THEDA BARA   ACTRESS, VAMP

She was divinely, hysterically, insanely malevolent.   **Bette Davis**

…a pyrogenic half pint…   **S.J. Perelman**

She is pretty bad, but not bad enough to be remembered always.

Alexander Woollcott

BRIGITTE BARDOT   ACTRESS

She eats when she is hungry and she makes love in the same matter-of-fact manner.   **Simone de Beauvoir**

A buxom milkmaid reminiscent of a cow wearing a girdle, and both have the same amount of acting talent. **Mr. (Earl) Blackwell**

I've always wanted to be Brigitte Bardot.   **Bob Dylan**

She used to sulk in the morning when I had not been nice to her in her dreams.   **Roger Vadim**

JOHN BARRYMORE ACTOR

It takes an earthquake to get Jack out of bed, a flood to make him wash and the United States Army to put him to work.
Lionel Barrymore (his brother)

Thank goodness I don't have to act with you anymore.
Katharine Hepburn

I always said that I'd like Barrymore's acting 'til the cows came home. Well, ladies and gentlemen, last night the cows came home.
George Jean Nathan

LIONEL BARRYMORE ACTOR

[He] uses words only to flog them. He makes them suffer.
John Barrymore

KIM BASINGER ACTRESS

Kim's as crazy as *any* person I've met.　　　　**Alec Baldwin**

The only time she was a problem was when she gave me a big hug and kiss at the end of a workday—and that problem went away in about half an hour.　　　　**Blake Edwards**

Kim Basinger is the most self-indulgent, dumb, most irritating person I've ever met. She's as dumb as a shoe.
Jonathan Van Meter

ANNE BAXTER ACTRESS

Her hair looks as if someone ran a brush through it and then said, "Oh, the hell with it."　　　　**Mr. (Earl) Blackwell**

WARREN BEATTY ACTOR, FILM DIRECTOR

He was insatiable. Three, four, five times a day was not unusual for him, and he was able to accept telephone calls at the same time.　　　　**Joan Collins**

I was seventeen and making *Shampoo* [when Warren] offered to relieve me of the huge burden of my virginity. Four times. That was the big offer. I decided against it. I decided for reality over anecdote. **Carrie Fisher**

So we had an affair. You must be pretty bad—I don't even remember you. **Bianca Jagger**

Am I just cynical, or does anyone else think the only reason Warren Beatty decided to have a child is so he can meet baby-sitters? **David Letterman**

Every time I go on a talk show I am invariably asked about Warren Beatty's sex life. I have a stock answer: "He should be in a jar at the Harvard Medical School." **Rex Reed**

I remember asking Warren Beatty if I could rehearse a scene just a little. So we rehearsed after work at night and we rehearsed Saturday and we rehearsed Sunday, and that was the *last* time I opened my mouth to Warren. **Maureen Stapleton**

He's the type of man who will end up dying in his own arms. **Mamie Van Doren**

JOHN BELUSHI COMEDIAN, ACTOR

A good man, but a bad boy. **Dan Aykroyd**

When *Back to the Future* first made it big, I kept a picture of John Belushi on my living room wall. That was to remind me what could happen if I lost my head and my values over this fame thing. **Michael J. Fox**

INGMAR BERGMAN FILM DIRECTOR

I just don't know what the hell he's after. **Frank Capra**

Do you know what Ingmar Bergman did at breakfast? He told his nightmares and then told me I had to act in them! I got another script from Ingmar in the mail and I returned it to him unopened and wrote, "Do your own nightmares!" **Liv Ullman**

INGRID BERGMAN ACTRESS

Too bad she's not queen of some country.

Goldie Hawn

I don't want to star opposite an unknown Swedish broad.

George Raft

SARAH BERNHARDT STAGE STAR

An empty cab drove up and Sarah Bernhardt got out.

Arthur "Bugs" Baer

The film audience could see her only as a figure of fun, a dumb creature jerking her sawdust heart around in a puppet world.

Alistair Cooke

Madame Bernhardt has the charm of a jolly maturity, rather spoilt and petulant, perhaps, but always ready with a sunshine-through-the-clouds smile if only she is made much of. Her dresses and diamonds, if not exactly splendid, are splendacious; her figure, far too scantily upholstered in the old days, is at its best; her complexion shows that she has not studied modern art in vain.

George Bernard Shaw

BERNARDO BERTOLUCCI FILM DIRECTOR

I don't think Bertolucci knew what *Last Tango in Paris* was about. And *I* didn't know what it was about. He went around telling everybody it was about his prick.

Marlon Brando

LINDA BLAIR ACTRESS

When I was your age, I was nineteen.

Victor Borge

HUMPHREY BOGART ACTOR

He was a pushover.

Lauren Bacall

Fame creates its own standard. A guy who twitches his lips is just another guy with a lip twitch—unless he's Humphrey Bogart.

Sammy Davis, Jr.

He was a real man—nothing feminine about him. He knew he was a natural aristocrat—better than anybody.

Katharine Hepburn

[I] hated that bastard.

William Holden

I have to be up early to make sure the set is ready for prematurely balding and aging actors like you.

Stanley Kramer

His first thought was, "Let's have a drink." His second was, "Now, who can we louse up today? Let's get started."

Earl Wilson

PETER BOGDANOVICH — FILM DIRECTOR

I never listened to his direction because I never liked it.

Cher

CLARA BOW — THE "IT" GIRL

Clara Bow had "It." She probably caught "It" from receiving too many passes from too many football players.

Susan Hayward

KENNETH BRANAGH — ACTOR, FILM DIRECTOR

I didn't know until later how like my father he is. It's extraordinary and weird. They're both kind of...walnutty. Like a walnut. Hard to crack. Rather suspicious.

Emma Thompson

MARLON BRANDO — ACTOR

I'd trade everything to be Marlon Brando.

Woody Allen

I came out here with one suit and everybody said I looked like a bum. Twenty years later Marlon Brando came out with only a sweatshirt and the town drooled over him. That shows how much Hollywood has progressed.

Humphrey Bogart

Actors like him are good but on the whole I do not enjoy actors who seek to commune with their armpits, so to speak.

Greer Garson

Hurricane Marlon is sweeping the country and I wish it were more than hot air.

Stanley Kauffman

He looked to me like a kid who delivers groceries.

Clifford Odets

Most of the time he sounds like he has a mouthful of wet toilet paper.

Rex Reed

...Marlon Brando in *Superman*. The greatest screen actor in the history of the cinema—perhaps—and he's running around with white hair and a Krypton suit. Just something wrong about that.

James Woods

CHARLES BRONSON   ACTOR

I think I'm in so many of his pictures because no other actress would work with him.

Jill Ireland

LOUISE BROOKS   ACTRESS

If I ever write a part for a cigar-store Indian, she'd get it.

Anita Loos

MEL BROOKS   FILM DIRECTOR, COMEDIAN

The public will never see him at his funniest and most intelligent. Melvin is at his best when he's with friends and in a raging jealousy over someone more successful.

Joseph Heller

Mel Brooks is sensual with me. He treats me like an uncle. A dirty uncle.

Madeline Kahn

The death of Hollywood is Mel Brooks and special effects. If Mel Brooks had come up in my time he wouldn't have qualified to be a busboy.

Joseph L. Mankiewicz

YUL BRYNNER   ACTOR

Yul Brynner was shorter. I suggested putting a little block under him. "You think I want to play it standing on a box? I'll show the world what a big horse you are!" I never had a complex about my height after that.

Ingrid Bergman

RICHARD BURTON   ACTOR

Richard Burton once drank a quart of brandy during his performance of *Hamlet* on Broadway. The only visible effect was that he played the last two acts as a homosexual.   **James Bacon**

There is no longer any novelty in watching the sad disintegration of his acting career.   **Roger Ebert**

Who could take that scruffy arrogant buffoon seriously?
Eddie Fisher

He has a terrific way with women. I don't think he has missed more than half a dozen.   **Fredric March**

Make up your mind, Richard Burton. A household word or a great actor.   **Laurence Olivier**

Richard Burton is so discriminating that he won't go to see a play with anybody in it but himself.   **Elizabeth Taylor**

JAMES CAGNEY   ACTOR

James Cagney rolled through the film like a very belligerent barrel.   **Noël Coward**

MRS. PATRICK CAMPBELL (BEATRICE STELLA TANNER)
STAGE ACTRESS

If only you could write a true book entitled *Why, Though I Was a Wonderful Actress, No Manager or Author Would Ever Engage Me Twice If He Could Possibly Help It*, it would be a best seller. But you couldn't. Besides, you don't know. I do.
George Bernard Shaw

An ego like a raging tooth.   **William Butler Yeats**

FRANK CAPRA   FILM DIRECTOR

I'd rather be Capra than God. If there *is* a Capra. **Garson Kanin**

CAPUCINE ACTRESS

Kissing you is like kissing the side of a beer bottle.

Laurence Harvey

JOHN CASSAVETES FILM DIRECTOR, ACTOR

As an artist I love him. As a husband I *hate* him. **Gena Rowlands**

CAROL CHANNING ACTRESS

She never just enters a room. Even when she comes out of the bathroom her husband applauds. **George Burns**

CHARLIE CHAPLIN COMEDIAN, ACTOR, FILM DIRECTOR

The son of a bitch is a ballet dancer! He's the best ballet dancer that ever lived, and if I get a good chance I'll strangle him with my bare hands. **W.C. Fields**

Chaplin is no businessman—all he knows is that he can't take anything less. **Samuel Goldwyn**

Sometimes I suspect that much of the trouble he's been in started the first time he read that he was a "sublime satirist" and a first-rate artist. He believed every word of it and tried to live and think accordingly. **Buster Keaton**

Chaplin is all content and little form. Nobody could have shot a film in a more pedestrian way than Chaplin. **Stanley Kubrick**

If people don't sit at Chaplin's feet, he goes out and stands where they're sitting. **Herman Mankiewicz**

That obstinate, suspicious, egocentric, maddening and lovable genius of a problem child. **Mary Pickford**

One of the worst appreciators of comedy outside of himself and his own genius. **James Thurber**

When he found a voice to say what was on his mind, he was like a child of eight writing lyrics for Beethoven's Ninth. **Billy Wilder**

CHEVY CHASE COMEDIAN, ACTOR

I said that I didn't think Chevy Chase could ad-lib a fart after a baked-bean dinner. **Johnny Carson**

Chevy Chase is pathetic. He's palling around on golf courses now with Gerald Ford, the doofus president he used to make fun of. **Howard Stern**

CHER ACTRESS, SINGER

…has had so much cosmetic surgery that for ease of maintenance many of her body parts are attached with velcro. **Dave Barry**

A bag of tattooed bones in a sequined slingshot. **Mr. (Earl) Blackwell**

I'd chuck it tomorrow if Cher called to do the act again. **Sonny Bono**

She's a little long in the tubes to be prancing around naked in public. **Carrie Fisher**

It must be tough having a beautiful mother like Cher and being named Chastity. I guess the only thing worse would be being beautiful and being named Slut. **Ava Gardner**

MAURICE CHEVALIER ACTOR, DANCER, SINGER

A great artiste but a small human being. **Josephine Baker**

He was sour, scowling and ill-humored, as well as a notorious tightwad. **James M. Cain**

MONTGOMERY CLIFT ACTOR

[It's] like he's got a Mixmaster up his ass and doesn't want anyone to know it. **Marlon Brando**

Mr. Montgomery Clift gives the performance of his career in *A Place In The Sun*, which is not saying a great deal since he had already demonstrated in *The Heiress* that he didn't belong on the same screen with first-class actors. **Raymond Chandler**

Working with Montgomery Clift was difficult because, you know, he was a Method actor and neurotic as well.   **Alfred Hitchcock**

He was full of all kinds of problems, many of them imaginary.

Myrna Loy

The only person I know who's in worse shape than I am.

Marilyn Monroe

GLENN CLOSE ACTRESS

She always looks like she has a secret.   **Michael Douglas**

HARRY COHN MOVIE PIONEER, COLUMBIA PICTURES FOUNDER

You had to stand in line to hate him.   **Hedda Hopper**

He was a great showman and he was a son of a bitch.

George Jessel

He liked to be the biggest bug in the manure pile.   **Elia Kazan**

I wish to be cremated when I die and my ashes to be thrown in Harry Cohn's face.   **Norman Krasna**

He had a sense of humor like an open grave.   **Frank Sinatra**

CLAUDETTE COLBERT ACTRESS

That French broad likes money.   **Harry Cohn**

I'd wring your neck, if you had one!   **Noël Coward**

RONALD COLMAN ACTOR

Ronald Colman is a gentleman. Yes, yes. So big deal. He's also a regular sleeping pill.   **Van Heflin**

SEAN CONNERY ACTOR

May I say, as long as actors are going into politics I wish for Christ's sake that Sean Connery would become king of Scotland.

John Huston

GARY COOPER `ACTOR`

When he puts his arms around me I feel like a horse.   **Clara Bow**

That guy just represents America to me. He's strong, he's able, he's kind, he wouldn't steal a penny from you, but if you cross his path, he'll kill you—or at least give you a punch in the mouth.
Frank Capra

One of the most beloved illiterates this country has ever known.
Carl Sandburg

He's got a reputation as a great actor just by thinking hard about the next line.   **King Vidor**

He had magic. The only time he was in trouble was when he tried to act.   **Fred Zinneman**

FRANCIS FORD COPPOLA `FILM DIRECTOR`

Coppola couldn't piss in a pot.   **Bob Hoskins**

Whatever Francis does for you always ends up benefitting Francis the most.   **George Lucas**

KEVIN COSTNER `ACTOR, FILM DIRECTOR`

This epic [*Dances with Wolves*] was made by a bland megalomaniac (the Indians should have named him Plays With Camera).
Pauline Kael

Kevin Costner has personality-minus.   **Madonna**

Mention his name around any woman between the ages of twenty and eighty-five and they drool. They love him. He's the ladies' man of the eighties—or the second half of the eighties—or the second half of '88—or the ladies' man du jour.   **Martin Mull**

When I look at a film of Kevin Costner's I fall asleep out of boredom.   **Mickey Rourke**

JOAN CRAWFORD ACTRESS

Judy Holliday is the funniest comedic actress in pictures, and Joan Crawford is the funniest dramatic actress.

Constance Bennett

I think she is a splendid actress but I'm a little repulsed by her shining lips, like balloon tires in wet weather. **John Betjeman**

She was radioactive with belief in herself. **Quentin Crisp**

Christ, you never know what size boobs that broad has strapped on! She must have a different set for each day of the week! She's supposed to be shriveling away, but her tits keep growing. I keep running into them like Hollywood Hills. **Bette Davis**

The best time I ever had with her was when I pushed her downstairs in *Baby Jane*. **Bette Davis**

There is not enough money in Hollywood to lure me into making another picture with Joan Crawford. And I like money.

Sterling Hayden

She's like that old joke about Philadelphia. First prize, four years with Joan. Second, eight. **Franchot Tone**

CHARLES CRICHTON FILM DIRECTOR

He's the only director I've ever worked with who's still trying to get over the impact of the talkies. **John Cleese**

HUME CRONYN ACTOR

When he's late for dinner I know he's either having an affair or is lying dead in the street. I always hope it's the street.

Jessica Tandy

BING CROSBY SINGER, ACTOR

He's the toppest...the peerest. **Louis Armstrong**

Bing Crosby sings like all people think they sing in the shower.

Dinah Shore

TOM CRUISE ACTOR

I don't need to be Tom Cruise. I just need to work forever.

Jodie Foster

...a kid off a Wheaties box.   **Oliver Stone**

You know, I've done seventy plays in my life, twenty-eight movies
and thirty-nine TV shows, and I think, "Couldn't I possibly at
least get a salary that matches Tom Cruise's per diem?"

James Woods

BILLY CRYSTAL COMEDIAN, ACTOR

Billy Crystal? I crap bigger than him.   **Jack Palance**

TONY CURTIS ACTOR

I shared drugs with my dad many times when I was in my twen-
ties. We had no relationship, really.   **Jamie Lee Curtis**

He is, in my book, a passionate amoeba.   **David Susskind**

The trouble with Tony Curtis is that he's interested only in tight
pants and wide billing.   **Billy Wilder**

MARION DAVIES ACTRESS

She has two expressions: joy and indigestion.   **Dorothy Parker**

BETTE DAVIS ACTRESS

Surely no one but a mother could have loved Bette Davis at the
height of her career.   **Brian Aherne**

Bette and I are very good friends. There's nothing I wouldn't say
to her face—both of them.   **Tallulah Bankhead**

Bette and I work differently. Bette screams, and I knit. While she
screamed, I knitted a scarf that stretched clear to Malibu!

Joan Crawford

She has as much sex appeal as Slim Summerville.   **Carl Laemmle**

I can't imagine any guy giving her a tumble.   **Carl Laemmle**

It is as though whenever she enters any room she is compelled to use her favorite silver screen expression, "What a dump."

Joshua Logan

You were very good playing a bitch-heroine, but you shouldn't win an award for playing yourself.   **Jack L. Warner**

DORIS DAY ACTRESS, SINGER

Just about the remotest person I know.   **Kirk Douglas**

You know, J.B. [Jut-Butt], we could play a nice game of bridge on your ass.   **Bob Hope**

No one realized that under all those dirndls lurked one of the wildest asses in Hollywood.   **Ross Hunter**

I knew her before she was a virgin.   **Oscar Levant**

We used to call her Miss Sparkle Plenty because she was so vivacious.   **Virginia Mayo**

Doris Day is one of the most difficult actresses I've met. She spent so much time crying.   **David Niven**

She thinks she doesn't get old. She told me once it was her cameraman who was getting older. She wanted me to fire him.

Joe Pasternak

JAMES DEAN ACTOR

If he'd have lived, they'd have discovered he wasn't a legend.

Humphrey Bogart

James Dean epitomized the very thing that's so campily respectable today: the male hustler. He had quite a sordid little reputation. I admire him immensely.   **David Bowie**

Intense, moody, incredible charisma. Short, myopic, not good-looking. You know who he was like? A young Woody Allen.

Joan Collins

Another dirty shirt-tail actor from New York.   **Hedda Hopper**

I don't mean to speak ill of the dead, but he was a prick...he was selfish and petulant, and believed his own press releases.
Rock Hudson

He was a hero to the people who saw him only as a little waif, when actually he was a pudding of hatred.   **Elia Kazan**

All in all, it was a hell of a headache to work with him.
George Stevens

OLIVIA DE HAVILLAND   ACTRESS

We're getting closer together as we get older, but there would be a slight problem of temperament. In fact, it would be bigger than Hiroshima.   **Joan Fontaine, her sister**

DOM DELUISE   ACTOR

One of the world's foremost chickens.   **Mike Douglas**

CECIL B. DEMILLE   FILM DIRECTOR, PRODUCER

I learned an awful lot from him by doing the opposite.
Howard Hawks

He made small-minded pictures on a big scale.   **Pauline Kael**

I never met such an egotist in my life. Even if he was wrong and knew it, once he said it it had to be.   **Arthur Miller**

When Mary [Pickford] found out about [his] flirtation she went quite mad. Unfaithful to HER? Off with his head.
Adela Rogers St. Johns

He wore baldness like an expensive hat, as though it were out of the question for him to have hair like other men.
Gloria Swanson

When I saw one of his pictures I wanted to quit the business.
King Vidor

CATHERINE DENEUVE ACTRESS

Catherine Deneuve is the man I've always wanted to be.

Gérard Depardieu

Catherine Deneuve is an iceberg. Gorgeous, but an iceberg. And her beauty is melting, melting, melting. **Steve McQueen**

She took the rough with the smooth with apparent serenity. I never noticed that she was quietly sharpening her claws.

Roger Vadim

ROBERT DE NIRO ACTOR

To me he's just an invisible man. He doesn't exist.

Truman Capote

…a class-A bastard. **Liza Minnelli**

Robert DeNiro is a very intense actor. He doesn't play joy very well. **Neil Simon**

Bobby needs somebody to watch over him. He doesn't even know enough to wear a coat in the wintertime. **Shelley Winters**

SANDY DENNIS ACTRESS

She has made an acting style out of postnasal drip. **Pauline Kael**

It should be added that she balanced her postnasal condition with something like prefrontal lobotomy, so that when she is not a walking catarrh she is a blithering imbecile. **John Simon**

JOHNNY DEPP ACTOR

Johnny's such a nice boy. If I worked with him again I'd have to cast him as a serial killer. **John Waters**

BO DEREK ACTRESS

She turned down the role of Helen Keller because she couldn't remember the lines. **Joan Rivers**

JOHN DEREK FILM DIRECTOR

It's only as a pornographer that he's a failure. He's hopeless as a filmmaker too, but probably no one cares.   **David Denby**

I have a feeling of permanence with John, but whenever I get tough or opinionated he jokes that he's going down to the high school.   **Bo Derek**

MARLENE DIETRICH ACTRESS

Miss Dietrich is not so much a performer as a one-woman environment.   **Vincent Canby**

The more she talks, the more you begin to respect Garbo.   **Rex Reed**

Marlene Dietrich's legs may be longer, but I have seven grand-children.   **Gloria Swanson**

WALT DISNEY ANIMATOR, BUSINESS EXECUTIVE

Disney, of course, has the best casting. If he doesn't like an actor he just tears him up.   **Alfred Hitchcock**

KIRK DOUGLAS ACTOR

Kirk never makes an effort towards people. He's pretty much wrapped up in himself.   **Doris Day**

He's wanted to be Burt Lancaster all his life.   **John Frankenheimer**

Kirk would be the first to tell you he's a difficult man. I would be the second.   **Burt Lancaster**

MICHAEL DOUGLAS ACTOR

If I'd known what a big shot Michael was going to be I would've been nicer to him as a kid.   **Kirk Douglas**

I was warned by everyone in Hollywood that Michael couldn't act.

Oliver Stone

RICHARD DREYFUSS ACTOR

Somebody called me the other day about going to a symposium on what it means to be an activist. I said, "Look, tell them I am too fucking active to do a symposium on what it means to be an activist." Let Richard Dreyfuss go and sit there and bullshit about it.

Susan Sarandon

KEIR DULLEA ACTOR

Keir Dullea and gone tomorrow.

Noël Coward

FAYE DUNAWAY ACTRESS

I'd say, "Faye, I want you to know exactly why I'm not with you in this particular instance." A waste of time. She'd always interrupt me in the middle of the sentence.

Jack Nicholson

She was a gigantic pain in the ass. She demonstrated certifiable proof of insanity.

Roman Polanski

SHELLEY DUVALL ACTRESS

Shelley Duvall is the worst and homeliest thing to hit the movies since Liza Minnelli.

John Simon

CLINT EASTWOOD ACTOR, FILM DIRECTOR

He isn't an actor, so one could hardly call him a bad actor. He'd have to do something before we could consider him bad at it.

Pauline Kael

We both have a particular audience that is loyal to us no matter what the critics say. With Clint, they want him to rip the bad guy's face off.

Burt Reynolds

NELSON EDDY SINGER, ACTOR

The ham of hams.

Allan Dwan

BLAKE EDWARDS FILM DIRECTOR

A man of many talents, all of them minor.   **Leslie Halliwell**

FRANCES FARMER ACTRESS

Cinderella goes back to the ashes on a liquor-slicked highway.
Louella Parsons

The nicest thing I can say about Frances Farmer is that she is
unbearable.   **William Wyler**

MIA FARROW ACTRESS

Trying to describe Mia is like trying to describe dust in a shaft of
sunlight. There are all those particles. Her conversation is clotted.   **Roddy McDowall**

FEDERICO FELLINI FILM DIRECTOR

His films are a small-town boy's dream of a big city...but he
shows dangerous signs of being a superlative artist with little to
say.   **Orson Welles**

SALLY FIELD ACTRESS

I certainly don't agree with a friend of mine who says that Miss
Field is simply a Mary Tyler Moore someone has stepped on.
Vincent Canby

W.C. FIELDS COMEDIAN, ACTOR

Bill never really wanted to hurt anybody. He just felt an obliga-
tion.   **Gregory La Cava**

There's no one in the world quite like Bill—thank God.
Mae West

EDDIE FISHER SINGER, ACTOR

...never very bright, and emotionally speaking he wasn't even
ready for his bar mitzvah at thirty.   **Rona Barrett**

The reason I drink is because when I'm sober, I think I'm Eddie Fisher.

Dean Martin

ERROL FLYNN ACTOR

The great thing about Errol was that you knew precisely where you were with him—because he *always* let you down.

David Niven

You know Flynn, he's either got to be fighting or fucking.

Jack L. Warner

JANE FONDA ACTRESS

...so obsessed with remaining inhumanly taut by working out ninety-two hours a day that it took her more than a decade to notice that she was married to a dweeb.

Dave Barry

Jane Fonda didn't get that terrific body from exercise. She got it from lifting all that money.

Joan Rivers

I would like to nominate Academy Award-winning actress Jane Fonda for a new award: the rottenest, most miserable performance by any one individual American in the history of our country.

Robert H. Steele

Unfortunately she's lost her sense of humor. One day I called her Jane of Arc. She didn't laugh at all.

Roger Vadim

I've known Jane since she was a French housewife.

Gore Vidal

The more you give in to her the more domineering she becomes.

Fred Zinneman

PETER FONDA ACTOR

I'm sorry, man, he just can't act.

Bruce Dern

HARRISON FORD ACTOR

He looks like he's carrying a gun even if he isn't.

Carrie Fisher

JOHN FORD FILM DIRECTOR

John is half-tyrant, half-revolutionary; half-saint, half-Satan; half-possible, half-impossible; half-genius, half-Irish.

Frank Capra

Actors were terrified of him because he liked to terrify them. He was a sadist.

John Carradine

Whatever John Ford wants, John Ford gets.

Edward G. Robinson

CLARK GABLE ACTOR

He used to claim he was very dull in bed.

Eve Arden

The best ears of our lives.

Milton Berle

He's the kind of guy who, if you say, "Hiya, Clark, how are ya?" is stuck for an answer.

Ava Gardner

Clark Gable's ears make him look like a taxicab with both doors open.

Howard Hughes

Listen, he's no Clark Gable at home.

Carole Lombard

Gable's ears stuck out like a couple of wind socks.

Jack L. Warner

GRETA GARBO ACTRESS

Every man's harmless fantasy mistress. She gave you the impression that if your imagination had to sin, it could at least congratulate itself on its impeccable taste.

Alistair Cooke

Garbo's temperament reflected the rain and gloom of the long dark Swedish winters.

Lillian Gish

Gary Cooper and Greta Garbo are the same person. After all, have you ever seen them in a movie together?

Ernst Lubitsch

A deer in the body of a woman, living resentfully in the Hollywood zoo.
Clare Booth Luce

Co-starring with Garbo hardly constituted an introduction.
Fredric March

I got into an elevator at MGM once and there in one of her famous men's hats was Garbo. I said hello, and when there was no reply I said, "Oh, sorry, I thought you were a fellow I knew."
Groucho Marx

AVA GARDNER ACTRESS

Ava's a *gent!*
George Cukor

Ava Gardner probably represented more tempestuous passion and sex appeal than one marriage could ever contain.
Kitty Kelley

A lady of strong passions, one of them rage.
Mickey Rooney

She was a goddess. I would stare at her, literally stare, in wonder.
Artie Shaw

Ava has been completely victimized by the kind of life she has led and as a result has become the kind of person she is today.
Artie Shaw

JOHN GARFIELD ACTOR

He had a penchant for picking up girls, sometimes two at a time, and a reputation as a demon lover. He died young, in bed, which was understandable.
Lana Turner

JUDY GARLAND ACTRESS, SINGER

I didn't know her well, but after watching her in action I didn't want to know her well.
Joan Crawford

Such a tragedy. Too much work, too much pressure, the wrong kind of people as husbands.   **Bing Crosby**

On one occasion when Judy Garland and I embraced each other, I felt it was such a unification of two great pill repositories that it must have been a peak in pharmaceutical history.   **Oscar Levant**

Her mental attitude may have been pathetic but it turned her into a great bore.   **Anita Loos**

Mother was the real-life Wicked Witch of the West. **Liza Minnelli**

TERI GARR ACTRESS

A major klutz.   **Liz Smith**

GREER GARSON ACTRESS

One of the most richly syllabled queenly horrors of Hollywood.
                                                  Pauline Kael

I gave up being serious about making pictures years ago, around the time I made a film with Greer Garson and she took 125 takes to say "No."   **Robert Mitchum**

RICHARD GERE ACTOR

He's got a pin-up image, which he hates. The only trouble is [that] whenever they ask him to take his trousers off, he does.
                                                  Michael Caine

People always want to know if it was love at first sight. I always say that it was interest at first sight.   **Cindy Crawford**

Richard Gere has taken his shirt off in every movie he's made. He's falling out of his clothes.   **Christopher Reeve**

For a while, that dropping-his-pants bit was an effective gimmick for the screen, but any way you measure it, his talent isn't big enough.   **Cornel Wilde**

MEL GIBSON ACTOR

Somebody should tell him [that] when he gets this famous he's supposed to be arrogant.   **Jamie Lee Curtis**

He did a lot of plays at drama school and every time without fail that he walked onstage, a ripple would run through the audience. It was quite odd. I always wanted to know how he did it: how does he do that ripple thing?   **Judy Davis**

If someone is looking for romance, this is a person you don't look to.   **Goldie Hawn**

Mel is the most gorgeous man I have ever seen.

Sigourney Weaver

JOHN GIELGUD ACTOR

Mr. Gielgud has the most meaningless legs imaginable.

Ivor Brown

A superb tenor voice, like a silver trumpet muffled in silk.

Alec Guinness

He was always coming out with these sweet, corny theatrical anecdotes, and he's got a sort of mucky sense of humor. I mean, everybody thinks he reads Chaucer all day and in fact he loves reading Harold Robbins.   **Dudley Moore**

I have always felt that Sir John Gielgud is the finest actor on earth from the neck up.   **Kenneth Tynan**

LILLIAN GISH SILENTS ACTRESS

...a sexless, silly antique.   **Louise Brooks**

JEAN-LUC GODARD FILM DIRECTOR

I once told Godard that he had something I wanted—freedom. He said, "You have something I want—money."   **Don Siegel**

Since Godard's films have nothing to say, perhaps we could have ninety minutes' silence instead of each of them.   **John Simon**

WHOOPI GOLDBERG ACTRESS, COMEDIENNE

I often ask myself if I have to be a thirty-year-old ex-junkie who lived in Berkeley and did stand-up comedy in Germany before I can get some respect. **Rae Dawn Chong**

She uses her huge eyes like a cartoon pussycat. **David Denby**

Do you know that when Whoopi Goldberg wears a dress, it's like drag. **Mildred Natwick**

I like Whoopi Goldberg. It's her hair that scares me. **Don Rickles**

SAMUEL GOLDWYN FILM PIONEER, PRODUCER

You always knew where you were with Goldwyn—nowhere. **F. Scott Fitzgerald**

I find I can live with Sam just as one lives with high blood pressure. **Robert Sherwood**

RUTH GORDON ACTRESS

When she does not have scenes to play in the theater she finds it necessary to create them in life. **Garson Kanin**

ELLIOTT GOULD ACTOR

He seemed to shock people every time he moved because beads of sweat sprayed out like little diamonds from his neck and arms. **Joshua Logan**

CARY GRANT ACTOR

The world has lost its quintessential romantic icon. **David Ansen**

They are trying to show he's a great lover but they'll never prove it to me. **Zsa Zsa Gabor**

He is personality functioning. **Katharine Hepburn**

D.W. GRIFFITH FILM PIONEER, PRODUCER, DIRECTOR

He was the first to photograph thought. **Cecil B. De Mille**

CHARLES GRODIN ACTOR

He keeps threatening to be funny but he rarely makes it.
Pauline Kael

TOM HANKS ACTOR

Tom Hanks is in what I'd call the Hat Pack. You know, a bunch of guys who occasionally wear hats and that's about as wild as they get. **Garry Marshall**

DARYL HANNAH ACTRESS

Daryl Hannah remains a rotten actress and still looks like a linebacker in a Lorelei wig. **John Simon**

JEAN HARLOW ACTRESS

The *t* [in my name] is silent—as in *Harlow*. **Margot Asquith**

There is no sign that her acting would ever have progressed beyond the scope of the restless shoulders and the protuberant breasts; her body technique was the gangster's technique—she toted a breast like a man totes a gun. **Graham Greene**

JULIE HARRIS ACTRESS

She scares small children. **Harry Cohn**

RICHARD HARRIS ACTOR

He's something of a fuck-up, no question. **Charlton Heston**

He hauls his surly carcass from movie to movie, being dismembered. I'd just as soon wait 'til he's finished. **Pauline Kael**

LAURENCE HARVEY ACTOR

After you've lived with Laurence Harvey, nothing in life is ever really too awful again.   **Hermione Baddeley**

Acting with Harvey is like acting by yourself—only worse.
                                                   Jane Fonda

The tales I can tell of working with him are too horrendous to repeat.   **Lee Remick**

GOLDIE HAWN ACTRESS

Goldie Hawn is as bright as a dim bulb.   **Totie Fields**

I can get jealous, but I don't see why Goldie would be with anyone other than me. I'm such a horse's ass when it comes to confidence in myself—I haven't met the guy she'd like more.
                                                   Kurt Russell

Goldie Hawn has a great body, and she's kept it. But she has the face of a chicken, and that plus her giggle is what kept her from being sexy or a sex symbol.   **Andy Warhol**

HELEN HAYES ACTRESS

Fallen archness.   **Franklin Pierce Adams**

PAUL HENREID ACTOR

He looks as though his idea of fun would be to find a nice cold damp grave and sit in it.   **Richard Winnington**

AUDREY HEPBURN ACTRESS

When she participates in the Academy Awards, she makes all those starlets look like tramps....If anyone said anything derogatory about her I'd push them in the river.   **Van Johnson**

A walking X-ray.   **Oscar Levant**

Audrey Hepburn is the patron saint of the anorexics.
                                                   Orson Welles

KATHARINE HEPBURN ACTRESS

She has a cheekbone like a death's head allied to a manner as sinister and aggressive as crossbones.   **James Agate**

She wasn't really standoffish. She ignored everyone equally.
Lucille Ball

She has a face that belongs to the sea and the wind, with large rocking-horse nostrils and teeth that you just know bite an apple every day.   **Cecil Beaton**

God, she's beautiful, God, she plays golf well, God, she can get anyone in the world on the phone, God, she knows what to do all the time, God, she wears clothes well.   **Joseph L. Mankiewicz**

Go to the Martin Beck Theater and watch Katharine Hepburn run the gamut-t-t of emotions from A to B.   **Dorothy Parker**

Not much meat on her, but what's there is cherce.
Spencer Tracy

Well, we just got used to working together. She butts in and I don't mind, and I pick it up when she leaves off. We just got used to working together, that's all.   **Spencer Tracy**

At the studio they called her Katharine of Arrogance. Not without reason, as I could tell you…but why bother?
Estelle Winwood

CHARLTON HESTON ACTOR

Scumbag.   **Ed Asner**

The trouble with him is he doesn't think he's just a hired actor like the rest of us. He thinks he's the entire production.
Richard Harris

Heston's the only man who could drop out of a cubic moon, he's so square.   **Richard Harris**

Charlton Heston wears a hairpiece. His character in *A Man for All Seasons* was bald. Instead of doing without his hairpiece, he put a bald pate *over* it. **Dustin Hoffman**

Hollywood—that's where they give Academy Awards to Charlton Heston for acting. **Shirley Knight**

Charlton Heston, a pretty fellow whom the moving pictures should exultantly capture without delay if they have any respect for the dramatic stage, duly adjusts his chemise so the audience may swoon over his expansive, hirsute chest and conducts his prize physique about the platform like a physical culture demonstrator. **George Jean Nathan**

This guy Charlton Heston is a nice fellow, but what a hamola. **Aldo Ray**

ALFRED HITCHCOCK | FILM DIRECTOR

Hitch is a gentleman farmer who raises goose flesh. **Ingrid Bergman**

One day he pulled up his shirt to show me his belly-button—which he didn't have. He'd had an operation and when they sewed him up they took it away. His belly-button was gone! **Karen Black**

The man with the navy-blue voice. **Barbara Harris**

Hitch relished scaring me. When we were making *Psycho*, he experimented with the mother's corpse, using me as his gauge. I would return from lunch, open the door to the dressing room and propped in my chair would be this hideous monstrosity. The horror in my scream, registered on his Richter scale, decided which dummy he'd use as the Madame. **Janet Leigh**

What did Hitchcock teach me? To be a puppet and not be creative. **Sylvia Sidney**

He looks like a little tubby pixie. **Jane Wyman**

DUSTIN HOFFMAN ACTOR

Better as a woman. If I were him I'd never get out of drag.

Mr. (Earl) Blackwell

I've always looked up to him, even though he *is* shorter.

Geena Davis

I told his wife I'd never work again for an Oscar winner who was shorter than the statue. **Larry Gelbart**

Why doesn't the boy just act? Why must he go through all this *sturm und drang?* **Laurence Olivier**

I'd give it [his Oscar for *Tootsie*] up if I could have back the nine months of my life I spent with Dustin making it. **Sydney Pollack**

There seemed to be a malevolence in him, a determination to make other human beings unhappy. **David Puttnam**

He looked about three feet tall, so dead serious, so humorless, so unkempt. **Katharine Ross**

…Hoffman's hesitancies of speech, his throatbound voice that has to struggle up past a colony of frogs, his eyes that crouch nervously in their sockets. **John Simon**

He came up to me and said, "I'm Dustin—burp—Hoffman," and he put his hand on my breast. What an obnoxious pig, I thought.

Meryl Streep

BOB HOSKINS ACTOR

A testicle with legs. **Pauline Kael**

ROCK HUDSON ACTOR

I call him Ernie because he's certainly no Rock. **Doris Day**

That big, lumpy Rock Hudson. **James Dean**

A miserable newspaper woman wrote something implying that Rock and I spent a lot of time together in San Francisco leather bars. I loved his response: "How in the hell did she find out so quick?"   **Blake Edwards**

Rock Hudson let his gay agent marry him off to his secretary because he didn't want people to get the right idea.

Anthony Perkins

HOWARD HUGHES FILMMAKER, RECLUSE

In his heyday he boasted of deflowering two hundred virgins in Hollywood. He must have got them all.   **Jimmy the Greek**

One day when he was eating a cookie he offered me a bite. Don't underestimate that. The poor guy's so frightened of germs, it could darn near have been a proposal.   **Jean Harlow**

A man whose life, more than that of any other man, resembles the most improbably Grade B Spectacular in glorious Vistavision.

John Keats

ANJELICA HUSTON ACTRESS

She's overpoweringly sexual; young men might find her frightening.   **Pauline Kael**

We were talking about Oscars. I didn't tell her she should have won, because the losers make all the money.   **Jack Nicholson**

JOHN HUSTON FILM DIRECTOR, ACTOR

John Huston told me early on, "I don't change anything. If that's the way they want it, that's the way they got it. They want bad pictures, we can make 'em bad, too. Cost a little more."

Robert Mitchum

John, if you weren't the son of my beloved friend Walter Huston, and if you weren't a brilliant writer, a fine actor and a magnificent director—you'd be nothing but a common drunk.

Gregory Ratoff

A Mephistopheles, an outrageously seductive, unfrocked cardinal, an amiable Count Dracula who drank only the best vintages of burgundy and never bared his teeth except to smile. He lives up to his living legend—and he lives it up. **Orson Welles**

JEREMY IRONS ACTOR

He's an iceberg with an accent. **Andy Warhol**

GLENDA JACKSON ACTRESS

Glenda Jackson has a face to launch a thousand dredgers.

Jack de Manio

In almost every play or film she inflicts her naked body on us which, considering its quality, is the supreme insult flung at the spectators. **John Simon**

AL JOLSON SINGER, ENTERTAINER

It was easy enough to make Jolson happy. You just had to cheer him for breakfast, applaud wildly for lunch and give him a standing ovation for dinner. **George Burns**

He was more than just a singer or an actor. He was an experience. **Eddie Cantor**

JAMES EARL JONES ACTOR

…less a star than he thinks. He's not nice, accommodating, sweet, talkative or cooperative. **Bryant Gumbel**

NEIL JORDAN FILM DIRECTOR, *THE CRYING GAME*

When you work with Neil you always get taken down strange roads. **Stephen Rea**

CAROL KANE ACTRESS

Her face is…uh…unique. **Diane Keaton**

BORIS KARLOFF ACTOR

Any face would have done as well on a big body, and any actor could have produced the short barks and guttural rumbles, the stiff, stuffed sawdust gestures, which was all his parts required of him.   **Graham Greene**

DIANE KEATON ACTRESS

Keaton believes in God. But she also thinks the radio works because there are tiny people inside it.   **Woody Allen**

GRACE KELLY ACTRESS

L'Altesse Frigidaire [Her Highness Frigidaire].   **Brigitte Bardot**

...a snow-covered volcano.   **Alfred Hitchcock**

DEBORAH KERR ACTRESS

Miss Kerr is a good actress. She is also unreasonably chaste.
                                                 Laurence Olivier

KLAUS KINSKI ACTOR

He's not aging well. The best thing to happen to his career is for him to die immediately.   **Werner Herzog**

He is so mad, terrible and vehement at the same time. Because of him, I never knew anything other than passion. When I began to meet other people I saw that it wasn't normal.   **Nastassja Kinski**

NASTASSJA KINSKI ACTRESS

Now Nastassja is passionate about being in movies. Indeed, she has nothing else on her mind, to the point of nausea.
                                                  Roman Polanski

STANLEY KUBRICK FILM DIRECTOR

Kubrick sounds a tough gig. I guess you'd need to be on steroids to work with him.   **Bill Murray**

Stanley's good on sound. So are a lot of directors but Stanley's good on designing a new harness. Stanley's good on the color of the mike. Stanley's good about the merchant he bought the mike from. Stanley's good about the merchant's daughter who needs some dental work. Stanley's good.   **Jack Nicholson**

He's an incredibly, depressingly serious man with this wild sense of humor....He's a perfectionist and he's always unhappy with anything that's set.   **George C. Scott**

ALAN LADD ACTOR

Hard, bitter and occasionally charming, he is after all a small boy's idea of a tough.   **Raymond Chandler**

I don't mean to be cruel, but Alan Ladd was not an actor's actor. But he was a very successful film star.   **Stewart Granger**

HEDY LAMARR ACTRESS

One evening when we were driving back from a concert I braked a little too quickly. Hedy became hysterical, claiming that I had purposely tried to throw her against the windshield because I was jealous of her beauty.   **Jean-Pierre Aumont**

DOROTHY LAMOUR ACTRESS

Dorothy, your hair looks like a cheap wig. Why do you wear it?   **Samuel Goldwyn**

BURT LANCASTER ACTOR

Before he can pick up an ashtray, he discusses his motivation for an hour or two. You want to say, "Just pick up the ashtray and shut up!"   **Jeanne Moreau**

JESSICA LANGE ACTRESS

Beautiful face, no brains, big bosoms.   **Dino De Laurentiis**

She is like a delicate fawn, but crossed with a Buick.

Jack Nicholson

CHARLES LAUGHTON ACTOR

He was the first actor I encountered who prepared to make a laughing entrance by going around doing *ha-ha!* sounds for hours.   **George Cukor**

You can't direct a Laughton picture. The best you can hope for is to referee.   **Alfred Hitchcock**

I confess I do not know what Mr. Laughton is up to, but I am sure I would hate to share a stage with it.   **Kenneth Tynan**

[He's] always hovering somewhere, waiting to be offended.
Peter Ustinov

He had a face that faintly resembled a large wad of cotton wool.
Josef Von Sternberg

VIVIEN LEIGH ACTRESS

She was often underrated because she was so beautiful.
George Cukor

JACK LEMMON ACTOR

When I did *The Happy Hooker Goes To Hollywood* my father told me, "That's one of the worst pieces of shit I've ever seen and you stunk."   **Chris Lemmon**

No one can convey specious cheerfulness better than Lemmon or make you feel more clammily sweaty under the collar.
John Simon

JERRY LEWIS COMEDIAN

One of the most hostile, unpleasant guys I've ever seen…through the years, I've seen him turn into this arrogant, sour, ceremonial, piously chauvinistic egomaniac. I'm just amazed at his behavior.
Elliott Gould

At some point he said to himself, "I'm extraordinary," like Chaplin. From then on, nobody could tell him anything. He knew it all. **Dean Martin**

Jerry Lewis hasn't made me laugh since he left Dean Martin.

Groucho Marx

KATHLEEN LLOYD `ACTRESS`

At UCLA she won the 1969 Hugh O'Brian Acting Award, which, I assume, is given annually for the best impersonation of Hugh O'Brian trying to act. **John Simon**

GINA LOLLOBRIGIDA `ACTRESS`

Gina's personality is limited. She is good playing a peasant but is incapable of playing a lady. **Sophia Loren**

She was a little stupid: she understood nothing of what she was doing and completely embarrassed the director.

Jean-Louis Trintignant

CAROLE LOMBARD `ACTRESS`

Carole Lombard was a wonderful girl. Swore like a man. Other women try, but she really did. **Fred MacMurray**

She was the only woman I've ever known who could say four-letter words and make it come out poetry. **William Wellman**

SOPHIA LOREN `ACTRESS`

Sophia Loren is the embodiment of what a woman should be— the epitome of femaleness. Most of the young people today are just ironing boards. **Rona Barrett**

Beautiful brown eyes set in a marvelously vulpine, almost satanic face. **Richard Burton**

Working with her is like being bombed by watermelons.

Alan Ladd

I do not talk about Sophia....She has a talent but it is not such a big talent. **Gina Lollobrigida**

PETER LORRE ACTOR

Those marbly pupils in the pasty spherical face are like the eye pieces of a microscope through which you can see laid flat on the slide the entangled mind of a man: love and lust, nobility and perversity, hatred of itself, and despair jumping up at you from the jelly. **Graham Greene**

GEORGE LUCAS FILM DIRECTOR

He reminded me a little bit of Walt Disney's version of a mad scientist. **Steven Spielberg**

SIDNEY LUMET FILM DIRECTOR

He's the only guy who could double-park in front of a whorehouse. He's that fast. **Paul Newman**

IDA LUPINO ACTRESS

Her familiar expression of strained intensity would be less quickly relieved by a merciful death than by Ex-Lax. **James Agee**

JEANETTE MacDONALD ACTRESS

That silly horse Jeanette MacDonald, yacking away at woodenpeg Eddy with all that glycerine running down her Max Factor. **Judy Garland**

ALI MacGRAW ACTRESS

We wanted to do a good man-woman story [*Chinatown*] and I had Ali in mind—at that time I was married to her. Well, in the interim she left me, so it wasn't for her. **Robert Evans**

...[a] truly terrible actress, of the nostril school. **Pauline Kael**

Ali MacGraw is proof that a great model is not necessarily a great—or even an average—actress. **Peter Sellers**

SHIRLEY MacLAINE ACTRESS

Her oars aren't touching the water these days. **Dean Martin**

She just behaved badly—like she was competing with me. I understand that Shirley grew up in a different era, when women had flesh under their fingernails from competing with one another, but I'm not like that. **Debra Winger**

HERMAN MANKIEWICZ SCREENWRITER

To know him was to like him. Not to know him was to love him.
Bert Kalmar

JAYNE MANSFIELD ACTRESS

Dramatic art in her opinion is knowing how to fill a sweater.
Bette Davis

Miss United Dairies herself. **David Niven**

FREDRIC MARCH ACTOR

He was able to do a very emotional scene with tears in his eyes and pinch my fanny at the same time. **Shelley Winters**

DEAN MARTIN SINGER, ACTOR

I wouldn't say Dean has a drinking problem, but his major concern in life is what wine goes with whiskey. **Joey Adams**

I still love Dean, but I don't like him anymore. **Jerry Lewis**

STEVE MARTIN ACTOR, COMEDIAN

I wish I was gay. I'd make it with Steve Martin.
Rodney Dangerfield

He doesn't own a second change of underwear.
Carl Reiner

LEE MARVIN ACTOR

Lee Moron.   **Marlon Brando**

Not since Attila the Hun swept across Europe leaving five hundred years of total blackness has there been a man like Lee Marvin.   **Joshua Logan**

THE MARX BROTHERS COMEDY TEAM

Working for the Marx Brothers was not unlike being chained to a galley car and lashed at ten-minute intervals.   **Dave Barry**

Cocoanuts introduced me to the Marx Brothers. *Cocoanuts* was a comedy, the Marx Brothers are comics, meeting them was a tragedy.   **George S. Kaufman**

CHICO MARX COMEDIAN, ACTOR

Now there sits a man with an open mind. You can feel the draft from here.   **Groucho Marx**

GROUCHO MARX COMEDIAN, ACTOR

The most embarrassingly unfunny comedian I have ever encountered.   **Kingsley Amis**

He's a male chauvinistic piglet.   **Betty Friedan**

...walked like an arthritic banana.   **Jack Paar**

The man was a major comedian, which is to say that he had the compassion of an icicle, the effrontery of a carnival shill and the generosity of a pawnbroker.   **S.J. Perelman**

HARPO MARX COMEDIAN, ACTOR

If he felt displeased by anything going on in front of him, he smiled, closed his eyes and fell asleep. He was able to fall asleep in a dentist's chair and remain asleep while having a tooth filled.
Ben Hecht

God bless you and keep you safe from anything as dangerous as knowledge.   **Alexander Woollcott**

WALTER MATTHAU `ACTOR`

Once seen, that antique-mapped face is never forgotten—a bloodhound with a head cold, a man who is simultaneously biting on a bad lobster and caught by the neck in lift-doors, a mad scientist's amalgam of Wallace Beery and Yogi Bear.   **Alan Brien**

He looks like a half-melted rubber bulldog.   **John Simon**

VICTOR MATURE `ACTOR`

I never go to movies where the hero's tits are bigger than the heroine's.   **Groucho Marx**

LOUIS B. MAYER `FILM PIONEER, PRODUCER`

...a hard-faced, badly-spoken and crass little man...[he] had the glibness of a self-taught evangelist and was mantled in the arrogance of success.   **Charles Bickford**

The reason so many people showed up at his funeral was because they wanted to make sure he was dead.   **Samuel Goldwyn**

Louis B. Mayer admires with his whole soul the drivel his underlings produce in his factory.   **Ben Hecht**

He had the memory of an elephant and the hide of an elephant. The only difference is that elephants are vegetarians and Mayer's diet was his fellow man.   **Herman Mankiewicz**

L.B. Mayer may be a shit, but not every shit is L.B. Mayer.
    Herman Mankiewicz

I wouldn't live in Hollywood if they elected me Mayer. **Billy Rose**

Put my ashes in a box and tell the messenger to bring them to Louis B. Mayer's office with a farewell message from me. Then when the messenger gets to Louis' desk I want him to open the box and blow the ashes in the bastard's face.   **Budd Schulberg**

MERCEDES McCAMBRIDGE `ACTRESS`

She smokes heavy. It sounds like she has three or four different screaming animals in her throat.   **William Friedkin**

STEVE McQUEEN ACTOR

His features resembled a fossilized washrag. **Alan Brien**

I can honestly say he's the most difficult actor I've ever worked with. **Norman Jewison**

One thing about Steve, he didn't like the women in his life to have balls. **Ali MacGraw**

A Steve McQueen performance just naturally lends itself to monotony. Steve doesn't bring much to the party.

Robert Mitchum

MELINA MERCOURI ACTRESS

Her blackly mascaraed eye-sockets gape like twin craters, unfortunately extinct. **John Simon**

BETTE MIDLER ACTRESS, SINGER

Secondhand Rose after a hurricane. **Mr. (Earl) Blackwell**

I'd let my wife, children and animals starve before I'd subject myself to something like [working with her] again. **Don Siegel**

SARAH MILES ACTRESS

She's a monster. If you think she's not strong, you'd better pay attention. **Robert Mitchum**

LIZA MINNELLI SINGER, ACTRESS

I always thought Miss Minnelli's face deserving—of first prize in the beagle category. **John Simon**

ROBERT MITCHUM ACTOR

Standing downwind, Mitchum is probably the sexiest man going today. **Joan Rivers**

MARILYN MONROE ACTRESS

There's a broad with her future behind her.   **Constance Bennett**

A fat cow.   **Harry Cohn**

She had no girdle on, her ass was hanging out. She is a disgrace to the industry.   **Joan Crawford**

...like kissing Hitler.   **Tony Curtis**

She's a plain kid. She'd give up the business if I asked her. She'd quit the movies in a minute.   **Joe DiMaggio**

She was good at playing abstract confusion in the same way a midget is good at being short.   **Clive James**

Marilyn was blowing take after take....Every man and woman on the set was loathing her. I said, "Don't worry, darling, that last one looked very good." She looked at me, puzzled, and said, "Worry about what?" I swore then that I'd never attribute human feelings to her again.   **Nunnally Johnson**

Copulation was, I'm sure, Marilyn's uncomplicated way of saying thank you.   **Nunnally Johnson**

Young lady, I think you're a case of arrested development. With your development, somebody's bound to get arrested.
                                                Groucho Marx

A professional amateur.   **Laurence Olivier**

A vacuum with nipples.   **Otto Preminger**

You know what they say about Marilyn Monroe—every man in the world wanted her. And all they had to do was ask. **Geraldo Rivera**

She had curves in places other women don't even have places.
                                                Cybill Shepherd

She has breasts like granite and a brain like Swiss cheese, full of holes. Extracting a performance from her is like pulling teeth.
                                                Billy Wilder

DUDLEY MOORE ACTOR

You are not very long for this earth. You are, in fact, very short
for this earth.   **Peter Cook**

ROBERT MORLEY ACTOR

Robert Morley is a legend in his own lunchtime.   **Rex Harrison**

ZERO MOSTEL ACTOR

[He] rolls his eyes on the screen as if he were running a bowling
alley in his skull.   **Andrew Sarris**

PAUL MUNI ACTOR

Paul Muni was a fascinating, exciting, attractive man—Jesus,
was he attractive!—and it was sad to see him slowly disappear
behind his elaborate make-up, his putty noses, his false lips, his
beards. One of the few funny things Jack Warner ever said was,
"Why are we paying him so much money when we can't find
him?"   **Bette Davis**

EDDIE MURPHY COMEDIAN, ACTOR

Despite all his success, Eddie acts like he's twenty-two years old.
His life is cars and girls, girls and cars. More cars. More girls.
                                                   Jamie Lee Curtis

Eddie can hear the rustle of nylon stockings at fifty yards.
                                                        Walter Hill

Hollywood Negro.   **Spike Lee**

BILL MURRAY COMEDIAN, ACTOR

He was an incredible slob. He wore shorts, wouldn't bathe for days.
He'd go around with six days' growth on his face.
                                                      Laraine Newman

JUDD NELSON ACTOR

Nelson gives a performance [in *The Billionaire Boys Club*] with flare: his eyes flare, his nostrils flare, his hair—if such a thing is possible—flares. His tonsils may have been flaring too, but at least you can't see them.

David Edelstein

PAUL NEWMAN ACTOR

Paul Newman's a great-looking ice cube.

Sal Mineo

I don't think Newman appreciated my scene [in *The Color of Money*] at all. In one take, my character had to proffer a joint to the young hero, so I think he didn't like it on those grounds. He kind of sat in the background and harrumph-harrumphed a lot.

Iggy Pop

He looks great and feels great, has lots of money, gives to good causes, is in love with his wife, races cars, is incredibly happy and still has a face....After having dinner with him, I wanted to shoot myself.

Robert Redford

I felt an enormous rivalry with Paul, although I wouldn't admit it to myself. In truth, I was always uncomfortable that Paul was so much bigger than I was. Uncomfortable and even angry because he was living my fantasy, being what I had always wanted to be: a star.

Joanne Woodward

JACK NICHOLSON ACTOR

Jack Nicholson's so rich, Jon Peters still cuts his hair.

Billy Crystal

He's fun because he doesn't make sense.

Carrie Fisher

...looks like a slightly seedy Eagle Scout who is always being stalked by a battalion of slightly aggressive field mice. **Rex Reed**

If Jack shit bricks, they'd give him an Oscar. **Mickey Rourke**

If he were here I'd ask him if I could lick his eyeballs.

Christian Slater

BRIGITTE NIELSEN ACTRESS

I despise heights. Maybe it's because of my second marriage. Brigitte was built like a mountain. Even Edmund Hillary couldn't climb her.   **Sylvester Stallone**

LESLIE NIELSEN ACTOR, COMEDIAN, WRITER

Leslie has high intelligence and hides it well.   **Robert Goulet**

A ten-year-old dipstick parading around as a genteel fifty-year-old.   **Jerry Zucker**

NICK NOLTE ACTOR

He's got much more sex appeal than I do.   **Warren Beatty**

Whenever Nick's around, there goes the neighborhood. He's just so terribly low-rent it's comical.   **Kate Nelligan**

CHUCK NORRIS MARTIAL ARTIST, ACTOR

I have always admired his training methods and devotion, but I didn't have the guts to tell him his acting stinks.

Bill Musselman

KIM NOVAK ACTRESS

I worked one day with her and I quit.   **Henry Hathaway**

When I was doing *Vertigo*, poor Kim Novak, bless her heart, said, "Mr. Hitchcock, what is my character feeling in relation to her surroundings?" There was silence on the set and Hitch said, "It's only a movie, for God's sakes." She never asked another question.   **James Stewart**

MERLE OBERON ACTRESS

She's still so beautiful. She says she's fifty-two. That would make her twelve years old when we made *The Private Life of Henry VIII* together.   **Binnie Barnes**

That Singapore streetwalker.   **Marlene Dietrich**

Amateur little bitch!   **Laurence Olivier**

MARGARET O'BRIEN ACTRESS

If that child had been born in the middle ages she'd have been burned as a witch.   **Lionel Barrymore**

MAUREEN O'HARA ACTRESS

She looks as though butter wouldn't melt in her mouth—or anywhere else.   **Elsa Lanchester**

LAURENCE OLIVIER ACTOR

I see Sir Laurence as a rhinoceros.   **Salvador Dali**

Larry Olivier is not an actor. He's a chameleon.   **Bette Davis**

Laurence Olivier doesn't look like an actor, either.
                                                        Gérard Depardieu

There have been times when I've been ashamed to take the money. But then I think of some of the movies that have given Olivier cash for his old age and I don't feel so bad.
                                                        Stewart Granger

I think that when Sir Laurence went into the theatre, motion pictures lost one of the great romantic stars of our time.
                                                        Alfred Hitchcock

TATUM O'NEAL ACTRESS

Tatum just wants to be treated like a little girl, which is what she is. Most people treat her like some kind of a freak, you know, who makes three hundred fifty thousand dollars a picture....I guess that is a freak.   **Walter Matthau**

I had to make this choice between Tatum and this girl—and I chose Farrah. Tatum made me choose. I said, "That's a bad idea. I sleep with this girl, Tatum. I don't sleep with you."
                                                        Ryan O'Neal

If ever things get real bad, I can live off her.   **Ryan O'Neal**

PETER O'TOOLE ACTOR

If you had been any prettier it would have been *Florence of Arabia*.
Noël Coward

AL PACINO ACTOR

He's virtually a specialist in showing the darker side of life.
Jane Fonda

It doesn't even look like the same face anymore. It's pasty, as if he'd vacated it.
Pauline Kael

LILLI PALMER ACTOR

I have never—with the possible exception of Claudette Colbert—worked with such a stupid bitch.
Noël Coward

ALAN PARKER FILM DIRECTOR

Parker is like a highbrow, left-wing Sylvester Stallone...he functions on the same Neanderthal level.
David Edelstein

SAM PECKINPAH FILM DIRECTOR

Film people are so fucking arrogant....We went to the set of one of his films, and oh dear, oh dear, I would have liked to have smashed him right in the fucking mouth.
Elton John

Peckinpah clearly doesn't lack talent; what he lacks is brains.
John Simon

SEAN PENN ACTOR

Every once in a while I wake up and go, "My God! I was married once. I was married, and he was the love of my life." It is like a death to deal with.
Madonna

He's a rarity as a father....It's all about purity, honesty and that cliché: unconditional love. I always knew he was that way, though. He was that way with his dogs.
Robin Wright

GEORGE PEPPARD ACTOR

He's arrogant—the sort of man who expects women to fall at his feet at the slightest command, who throws his weight around. He gives the impression that he's the star, what he says goes and that nobody else is very important. **Joan Collins**

ANTHONY PERKINS ACTOR

I think he'd do well to spend a summer on a ranch. **Gary Cooper**

To me he was a leading man. But he'll always be remembered as Norman. People won't let him be anything else. **Janet Leigh**

VALERIE PERRINE ACTRESS

She looks like the bride of Frankenstein doing the Ziegfeld Follies. **Mr. (Earl) Blackwell**

MICHELLE PFEIFFER ACTRESS

What Michelle Pfeiffer needs is a swift kick in the ass... she should stop torturing herself by whining about the bad stuff and get down on her knees and thank God for what she's got. **Melissa Gilbert**

I think it's a real ability to be ugly and unattractive. I think I can be beautiful and I can be ugly. Michelle Pfeiffer can't be ugly. **Juliette Lewis**

MARY PICKFORD ACTRESS

She was the girl every young man wanted to have—as his sister. **Alistair Cooke**

It took longer to make one of Mary's contracts than it did to make one of Mary's pictures. **Samuel Goldwyn**

You're too little and too fat, but I might give you a job. **D.W. Griffith**

Say anything you like, but don't say I want to work. That sounds like Mary Pickford, that prissy bitch. **Mabel Normand**

ROMAN POLANSKI FILM DIRECTOR

As a director he was ten times more wonderful than as a lover.

Nastassja Kinski

OTTO PREMINGER FILM DIRECTOR

I was warned about him—but could anybody really be *that* bad?
Yeah, they could.

Dyan Cannon

Otto Preminger was a hard-ass director before anyone knew that
Preminger wasn't a skin disease.

Jerry Lewis

He's one of that old school of tyrannical directors. He believes that real blood on the actors is better than make-up.

Robert Stack

I thank God that neither I nor any member of my family will
ever be so hard up that we have to work for Otto Preminger.

Lana Turner

I hear Otto Preminger's on holiday. In Auschwitz.　**Billy Wilder**

DENNIS QUAID ACTOR

A giant pain in the ass.

Jim McBride

ANTHONY QUINN ACTOR

I found out with Tony Quinn, who's inclined to be dreadfully
flamboyant and overdo things terribly if you let him, the way
to get a good performance is to goad him to the point of tears,
be nasty to him. If you let him take over, you're dead.

Edward Dmytryk

"I want to impregnate every woman in the world," he once told
me, though I didn't realize until later how literally he meant it.

Ruth Warrick

GEORGE RAFT ACTOR

When they make a man better than George Raft, I'll make him
too.

Mae West

CLAUDE RAINS ACTOR

He was a great influence on me. I don't know what happened to him. I think he failed and went to America.   **John Gielgud**

BASIL RATHBONE ACTOR

Two profiles pasted together.   **Dorothy Parker**

ROBERT REDFORD ACTOR, FILM DIRECTOR

I can't stand around like Redford. I'm not that narcissistic. Not that photogenic, either.   **William Devane**

Secretly, I think Bob is afraid of women. He likes to tell them what to do. He likes them to be subservient. He treated me as if I were an extra or something.   **Jane Fonda**

Redford is a dangerous man to let loose on the streets. He has holes in his head, he should be arrested.   **George Roy Hill**

He has turned almost alarmingly blond—he's gone past platinum, he must be plutonium; his hair is coordinated with his teeth.
          Pauline Kael

I wish I looked like Robert Redford and had a twelve-inch cock, but that isn't the way it worked out, okay?   **Kurt Russell**

Well, at least he has finally found his true love. What a pity he can't marry himself.   **Frank Sinatra**

Poor little man. They made him out of lemon Jell-O and there he is.   **Adela Rogers St. Johns**

VANESSA REDGRAVE ACTRESS

Some Trotskyite. She travels by Rolls Royce.   **Robert Duvall**

She knocked on my hotel room door to sell me a socialist newspaper for twenty-five cents...Vanessa Redgrave going door-to-door selling newspapers! Sunday morning at ten o'clock! I mean, I asked if she had the *New York Times* as well, but she didn't.
          Melanie Mayron

It reminds me of President Jimmy Carter and brother Billy. I'm no president and she's not Billy, but nonetheless...there's a sense of constant embarrassment which you must somehow endure.

Lynn Redgrave

This is a soul under perpetual migraine attack. **Richard Schickel**

CHRISTOPHER REEVE ACTOR

I can tell you that Christopher Reeve is not homosexual. When we kissed in *Deathtrap* he didn't close his eyes.   **Michael Caine**

BURT REYNOLDS ACTOR

Burt Reynolds once asked me out. I was in his room.

Phyllis Diller

Burt, in my book you have the sexual attractiveness of a dentist's drill.   **Don Rickles**

DIANA RIGG ACTRESS

Diana Rigg is built like a brick mausoleum with insufficient flying buttresses.   **John Simon**

ERIC ROBERTS ACTOR

For as many people I meet who love Eric Roberts, I meet just as many who think he's a jerk.   **Julia Roberts**

JULIA ROBERTS ACTRESS

Take away Julia Roberts's wild mane of hair and all those teeth and those elastic lips and what've you got? A pony! **Joyce Haber**

EDWARD G. ROBINSON ACTOR

What Einstein was to physics, what Babe Ruth was to home runs, what Emily Post was to table manners—that's what Edward G. Robinson was to dying like a dirty rat.   **Russell Baker**

GINGER ROGERS ACTRESS, DANCER

She may have faked a little, but we knew we had a good thing going.   **Fred Astaire**

She has a little love for a lot of people but not a lot for anybody.
George Gershwin

Fellow actor made a picture with Ginger, came to me and said, "She's not very easy to know, is she?" I said, "Not if you're lucky, old man."   **Cary Grant**

All Ginger Rogers was interested in was the dough-re-mi on the dotted line.   **Louella Parsons**

MICKEY ROONEY ACTOR

His favorite exercise is climbing tall people.   **Phyllis Diller**

MICKEY ROURKE ACTOR

...incredibly boring.   **Jacqueline Bisset**

JANE RUSSELL ACTRESS

Don't let her fool you. Tangle with her and she'll shingle your attic.   **Bob Hope**

There are two good reasons why men go to see her. Those are enough.   **Howard Hughes**

KEN RUSSELL FILM DIRECTOR

An arrogant, self-centered, petulant individual. I don't say this in any demeaning way.   **Bob Guccione**

KURT RUSSELL ACTOR

The attraction is not specifically sexual.   **Goldie Hawn**

WINONA RYDER ACTRESS

It became such a public thing…you're taking a squirt and some guy walks up to you and says, "Hey! How's Winona?" I mean, huh? You're there with your Johnson in your hand. It takes everything, every inch of strength not to turn around and pee on him.
Johnny Depp

GEORGE SANDERS ACTOR

We were both in love with him…I fell out of love with him, but he didn't.
Zsa Zsa Gabor

ARNOLD SCHWARZENEGGER ACTOR, BODYBUILDER

…a man whose chest is bigger than Madonna's.
Billy Crystal

He has so many muscles that he has to make an appointment to move his fingers.
Phyllis Diller

Arnold Schwarzenegger looks like a condom full of walnuts.
Clive James

GEORGE C. SCOTT ACTOR

Fine actor. Big drinker. Wife-beater. What else do you want to know?
Colleen Dewhurst

One of the best actors alive. But my opinion of him as an actor is much higher than my opinion of him as a man.
John Huston

RIDLEY SCOTT FILM DIRECTOR

Ridley Scott is mad, a force of nature. If I were a woman I would have made love with him.
Gérard Depardieu

PETER SELLERS ACTOR

As a man he was abject, probably his own worst enemy, although there was plenty of competition.
Roy Boulting

I would squirm with embarrassment at the demeaning lengths he would go to in order to ingratiate himself with the Royal Family.
Britt Ekland

He was not a genius, Sellers, he was a freak. **Spike Milligan**

Pete had an extraordinary sense of not being there. He genuinely felt that when he went into a room no one could see him.
Peter O'Toole

Talk about unprofessional rat finks. **Billy Wilder**

DAVID O. SELZNICK FILM PRODUCER

A typical Hollywood combination of oafishness and sophistication.
John Houseman

OMAR SHARIF ACTOR

His lips quiver with fake sensitivity while his voice drips genuine molasses, and his calorific regard could still, as in *Zhivago*, melt all the snows of Russia. As an actor, he is of no earthly use; perhaps the navy could use him as an icebreaker. **John Simon**

NORMA SHEARER ACTRESS

Oh, Mr. Thalberg, I've just met that extraordinary wife of yours with the teensy-weensy little eyes! **Mrs. Patrick Campbell**

I love to play bitches and she certainly helped me in the part.
Joan Crawford

A dead fish. **Marlene Dietrich**

A face unclouded by thought. **Lillian Hellman**

CYBILL SHEPHERD ACTRESS

Well, Bogdanovich is truly in love with Miss Shepherd, so one cannot call his slapping her into the lead of almost every one of his films the casting-couch approach; yet even those crude old-time producers who did have the crassness to use that method at least had the good sense to cast the girl, not the couch. **John Simon**

BROOKE SHIELDS ACTRESS, MODEL

Brooke Shields was posing nude long before I was.

Susan Sarandon

The Russians love Brooke Shields because her eyebrows remind them of Leonid Brezhnev. **Robin Williams**

[Directing her in *Endless Love* was] like cracking the whip at a limping horse. **Franco Zefferelli**

TALIA SHIRE ACTRESS

The only horrifying thing about [*The Prophecy*, a horror film] was—you guessed it—watching Talia Shire overact.

Rona Barrett

STEVEN SPIELBERG FILM DIRECTOR

Steven Spielberg doesn't know anything about actors, that's obvious. **Bruce Dern**

I'd like to make Steven Spielberg my slave and have him make any movie I wanted. **Sean Young**

SYLVESTER STALLONE ACTOR

There was a great headline in the paper down south the other day: "Stallone Still a Jerk." **Bryant Gumbel**

Sly Stallone is five-seven, I believe. Shorter than you'd think— not just short on talent. **Burt Lancaster**

I don't know what it is with him. He's got bulletproof glass in [his house] windows and at night there are so many spotlights turned on, the house looks like a damned spaceship. He's got two body-guards who look exactly like him walking around on the beach, so I guess he figures that cuts the odds of being assassinated to one in three. **Jack Lemmon**

Rocky III—surprisingly, he plays a *boxer* in this one. **Jay Leno**

Whatever he does, it always comes out wrong.

Arnold Schwarzenegger

Sylvester Stallone, who has never been successful in anything but a *Rocky* movie, will probably have made *Rocky MCMLXXXVIII* by 1989.

Gene Shalit

BARBARA STANWYCK ACTRESS

...Barbara Stanwyck who, when we were waiting to go into our scenes for *The Bride Wore Boots*, would whisper, "Come on, Bob. You know you'd like to fuck me. Admit it."

Robert Cummings

I once asked Barbara Stanwyck the secret of acting. She said, "Just be truthful—and if you can fake that, you've got it made."

Fred MacMurray

Barbara Stanwyck is my favorite. My God, I could just sit and dream of being married to her, having a little cottage out in the hills, vines around the door. I'd come home from the office tired and weary, and I'd be met by Barbara, walking through the door holding an apple pie she had cooked herself. And wearing no drawers.

Herman Mankiewicz

ROD STEIGER ACTOR

Rod Steiger's the worst actor that ever lived. The very name makes me throw up. He's so terrible. He's one of the world's worst hams. A real *jambon*.

Truman Capote

JAMES STEWART ACTOR

Jimmy Stewart is sort of square. Even in the early days he told me his idea of a romantic evening was soft lights, sweet music, champagne...no girl—just soft lights, sweet music and champagne.

Lucille Ball

If Bess and I had a son, we'd want him to be just like Jimmy Stewart.

Harry S Truman

OLIVER STONE FILM DIRECTOR

He has a great ability to piss you off.   **Johnny Depp**

You could plug Oliver into New York and he would power the city for two weeks.   **Gary Oldman**

Oliver Stone I don't like. But then, nobody likes Oliver. He's just an aggressive man, like me. But he hasn't my sense of humor.
                    Alan Parker

SHARON STONE ACTRESS

So goddamned mean—when she's angry she knows how to say things that really hurt.   **Paul Verhoeven**

MERYL STREEP ACTRESS

Her nose, that red thin sharp snout—it reminds you of an anteater.   **Truman Capote**

Meryl Streep is an acting machine in the same sense that a shark is a killing machine.   **Cher**

In this interview she was agonizing about having to meet the press. She was moaning that she didn't want a lot of people around. And I wanted to ask her, "Then why the hell are you an actress?" They're so damned sincere these days.   **George Cukor**

People are beginning to wonder if she can talk normal.
                    Geraldine Page

If her household runs as perfectly as her press would have us believe, I'll slash my throat.   **Susan Sarandon**

I can't say anything bad about Meryl Streep—and I love to say bad things about people.   **James Woods**

PRESTON STURGES FILM DIRECTOR, PLAYWRIGHT

I never could make a good film without a good writer—but neither could Preston Sturges. Only he had one with him all the time.   **William Wyler**

DONALD SUTHERLAND ACTOR

What a malodorous actor Sutherland has rapidly become: when he is not insanely overacting…he is equally maniacally underacting.

John Simon

GLORIA SWANSON ACTRESS

Damned if she didn't keep on getting married! I got her into an awful bad habit.

Wallace Beery

What'd you get that [Oscar] for, bowling?

José Ferrer

ELIZABETH TAYLOR ACTRESS

In tight sweaters and skirts she looks like a chain of link sausages.

Mr. (Earl) Blackwell

She has a double chin and an overdeveloped chest and she's rather short in the leg. So I can hardly describe her as the most beautiful creature I've ever seen.

Richard Burton

Our love is so furious that we burn each other out.

Richard Burton

I got so sick of starry-eyed close-ups of Elizabeth Taylor that I could have gagged.

Raymond Chandler

…never fails to try to con my diamond rings from me.

Sammy Davis, Jr.

All my life I wanted to look like Elizabeth Taylor. Now I find that Liz Taylor is beginning to look like me.

Divine

Sympathy would be on my side if the people knew the whole story of our marriage.

Eddie Fisher

When Elizabeth Taylor meets a man she takes him and squeezes the life out of him and then throws away the pulp.

Eddie Fisher's mother

Any man who hasn't fantasized about Elizabeth Taylor is either a homosexual or an agent.

Buddy Hackett

Let's face it, Elizabeth Taylor's last marriage was all about selling perfume because it's hard to sell perfume when you're a fat old spinster.   **John Lydon (Johnny Rotten)**

She should get a divorce and settle down.   **Jack Paar**

Wobbling her enormous derriere across the screen...and saying lines like: "I'm the biggest mother of them all" inspires pity instead of laughs. She has been announcing plans to retire from the screen. Now is as good a time as any.   **Rex Reed**

She's so fat, she's my two best friends.   **Joan Rivers**

When I took her to Sea World and Shamu the Whale jumped out of the water, she asked if it came with vegetables.   **Joan Rivers**

Elizabeth and I have a lot in common. We both like jewelry—it's just a question of size. We also both have this thing about actors. And again, it's just a question of size.   **Dinah Shore**

Just how garish her commonplace accent, squeakily shrill voice, and the childish petulance with which she delivers her lines are, my pen is neither scratchy nor leaky enough to convey.
                                                            John Simon

It would be very glamorous to be reincarnated as a great big ring on Liz Taylor's finger.   **Andy Warhol**

The way things are going I'd be more interested in seeing Cleopatra play the life of Elizabeth Taylor.   **Earl Wilson**

SHIRLEY TEMPLE ACTRESS, DIPLOMAT

A swaggering, tough little slut.   **Louise Brooks**

Shirley Temple had charisma as a child. But it cleared up as an adult.   **Totie Fields**

Acting is the most minor of gifts and not a very high-class way to earn a living. After all, Shirley Temple could do it at the age of four.   **Katharine Hepburn**

Don't bother about me. *The Grapes of Wrath* is unimportant compared to Shirley Temple's tooth.   **John Steinbeck**

A fifty-year-old midget.   **Mae West**

EMMA THOMPSON ACTRESS

Emma Thompson is one of my favorite actresses. I'm tired of seeing pretty young things giggle around.   **Mary-Louise Parker**

MIKE TODD FILM PRODUCER

I was hag-ridden by an indescribable megalomaniac named Mike Todd, a combination of Quasimodo and P.T. Barnum.
                                                    S.J. Perelman

SPENCER TRACY ACTOR

Spencer does it, that's all. Feels it. Says it. Talks. Listens. He means what he says when he says it, and if you think that's easy, try it.   **Humphrey Bogart**

To most men I'm a nuisance because I'm so busy I get to be a pest, but Spencer is so masculine that once in a while he rather smashes me down, and there's something nice about me when I'm smashed down.   **Katharine Hepburn**

It was always Tracy and Hepburn. I chided him once about his insistence on first billing. "Why not?" he asked. "Well, after all," I argued, "she's the lady. You're the man. Ladies first?" He said, "This is a movie, chowderhead, not a lifeboat."   **Garson Kanin**

HERBERT BEERBOHM TREE STAGE ACTOR, PRODUCER, PLAYWRIGHT

Do you know how they are going to decide the Shakespeare-Bacon dispute? They are going to dig up Shakespeare and dig up Bacon; they are going to set their coffins side by side, and they are going to get Tree to recite *Hamlet* to them. And the one who turns in his coffin will be the author of the play.   **W.S. Gilbert**

FRANÇOIS TRUFFAUT FILM DIRECTOR

He's now making the sort of films he used to rail against when he was a critic. **Claude Chabrol**

KATHLEEN TURNER ACTRESS

Kathleen Turner's okay in stills. When she talks and moves about, she reminds me of someone who works in a supermarket. **Ann Sothern**

LANA TURNER ACTRESS

Lana Turner is to an evening gown what Frank Lloyd Wright is to a pile of lumber. **Rex Harrison**

She is not even an actress...only a trollop. **Gloria Swanson**

...couldn't act her way out of her form-fitting cashmeres. **Tennessee Williams**

BRENDA VACCARO ACTRESS

With the exception of Sandy Dennis, there is no more irritatingly unfeminine actress around these days than Miss Vaccaro, a cube-shaped creature who comes across as a dikey Kewpie doll. **John Simon**

RUDOLPH VALENTINO ACTOR

Rudolph Valentino was catnip to women. **H.L. Mencken**

His acting is largely confined to protruding his large, almost occult eyes until the vast areas of white are visible, drawing back the lips of his wide, sensuous mouth to bare his gleaming teeth, and flaring his nostrils. **Adolph Zukor**

MAMIE VAN DOREN ACTRESS

Someone like Bette Davis or Barbara Stanwyck will keep going long after all the Mamie Van Dorens are faded mammaries. **Thelma Ritter**

ERICH VON STROHEIM FILM DIRECTOR, ACTOR

Von Stroheim was the greatest director in the world....But he was impossible, a crazy artist. If he had only been ten percent less himself and ten percent more reasonable, we would still be making pictures together.

Louis B. Mayer

He was a short man, almost squat, with a vulpine smirk that told you as soon as his image flashed on to the screen that no wife or bankroll must be left unguarded.

S.J. Perelman

RAOUL WALSH FILM DIRECTOR

To Raoul Walsh a tender love scene is burning down a whorehouse.

Jack L. Warner

JACK L. WARNER FILM EXECUTIVE

A man who would rather tell a bad joke than make a good movie.

Jack Benny

I can't see what J.W. can do with an Oscar. It can't say yes.

Al Jolson

Working for Warner Bros. is like fucking a porcupine. It's a hundred pricks against one.

Wilson Mizner

He bore no grudge against those he had wronged.

Simone Signoret

ETHEL WATERS ACTRESS, SINGER

She was a very sad person. Between scenes she sat all alone in her dressing room, listening to her old phonograph records.

Fred Zinneman

JOHN WAYNE ACTOR

...bigger than life in his performance—and often when he didn't have to be.

Katharine Hepburn

Great legs and tight buttocks, a real great seat, and small, sensitive feet.

Katharine Hepburn

I love John Wayne, but *Sands of Iwo Jima* sent me to Vietnam believing that it was exciting and I could make a man out of myself. I don't believe John Wayne ever went to war.

Oliver Stone

He is as tough as an old nut and as soft as a yellow ribbon.

Elizabeth Taylor

He walks like a fairy. He's the only man in the world who can do that.

William Wellman

SIGOURNEY WEAVER ACTRESS

Sigourney Weaver complains that she's not making as much money as Paul Newman. Well, some of us are not making as much as she is and we're just as good.

Whoopi Goldberg

RAQUEL WELCH ACTRESS

A moron with less on.

Totie Fields

I have never met anyone so badly behaved.

James Mason

She's one of the few actresses in Hollywood history who looks more animated in still photographs than she does on the screen.

Michael Medved

It was like talking to Hitler.

Iggy Pop

You have the best shoulders—gee!

Andy Warhol

TUESDAY WELD ACTRESS

What turns me on [is]...Tuesday Weld in a dirty slip, drinking beer.

Alice Cooper

ORSON WELLES FILM DIRECTOR, ACTOR

An active loafer, a wise madman.

Jean Cocteau

I know little about Orson's childhood and seriously doubt if he ever was a child.

Joseph Cotten

When I talk to him, I feel like a plant that's been watered.

Marlene Dietrich

...[he] particularly loved the ideas he took from me.

D.W. Griffith

By the sixties he was encased in make-up and his own fat, like a huge operatic version of W.C. Fields.   **Pauline Kael**

There but for the grace of God goes God.   **Herman Mankiewicz**

He has a voice of bottled thunder, so deeply encasked that one thinks of those liquor advertisements which boast that not a drop is sold 'til it's seven years old.   **Kenneth Tynan**

WILLIAM WELLMAN FILM DIRECTOR

...a tough little bastard.   **James Mason**

MAE WEST ACTRESS

A plumber's idea of Cleopatra.   **W.C. Fields**

...seductive and reeling motions reminiscent of an overfed python.   **Graham Greene**

She stole everything but the cameras.   **George Raft**

I told her that she was one of the three greatest talents ever to come out of the movies, the other two being W.C. Fields and Chaplin. She said, "Umm, well, I don't know about Fields."

Tennessee Williams

RICHARD WIDMARK ACTOR

It is clear that murder is one of the kindest things he is capable of.   **James Agee**

BILLY WILDER FILM DIRECTOR

His critiques of films are subtle and can be very amusing, especially of the ones he hasn't seen.   **David Hockney**

Beneath Billy Wilder's aggressive gruff exterior is pure Brillo.

Harry Kurnitz

You should be tarred and feathered and run out of Hollywood.

Louis B. Mayer

GENE WILDER ACTOR

One day God said, "Let there be prey," and he created pigeons, rabbits, lambs and Gene Wilder.   **Mel Brooks**

ESTHER WILLIAMS ACTRESS

Wet, she was a star.   **Joe Pasternak**

I can't honestly say that Esther Williams ever acted in an Andy Hardy picture, but she swam in one.   **Mickey Rooney**

BRUCE WILLIS ACTOR

The only reason I resent Bruce Willis is that he makes so much more money than me.   **Cybill Shepherd**

SHELLEY WINTERS ACTRESS

Well, if I'm your favorite author, then you really must be from Hollywood because that means you're practically illiterate.

Dorothy Parker

NATALIE WOOD ACTRESS

Natalie Wood is built like a brick dollhouse.   **Harry Kurnitz**

JAMES WOODS ACTOR

Woods couldn't have a consistent relationship with a doorknob.

Sean Young

God would have been merciful if he had given him a little teeny penis so that he could get on with his life.   **Sean Young**

JOANNE WOODWARD ACTRESS

I have a steak at home, why should I go out for a hamburger?

Paul Newman

FAY WRAY ACTRESS

During a dramatic episode in which a certain Miss Wray lay gibbering across Mr. Kong's wrist, my companion, in a voice shrill with irritation, cried out, "I can't think what he sees in her."

Quentin Crisp

WILLIAM WYLER FILM DIRECTOR

Doing a picture with Willie is like getting the works at a Turkish bath. You damn near drown, but you come out smelling like a rose.

Charlton Heston

LORETTA YOUNG ACTRESS

Whatever it is this actress never had, she still hasn't got it.

Bosley Crowther

SUSANNAH YORK ACTRESS

Susannah was the personification of uninformed arrogance of youth.

John Huston

SEAN YOUNG ACTRESS

Does the word *nightmare* mean anything to you?   **James Woods**

DARRYL F. ZANUCK FILM PRODUCER

He has so many yes-men following him around the studio, he ought to put out his hand when he makes a sharp turn. **Fred Allen**

Well, goodbye, Mr. Zanuck. And let me tell you it certainly has been a pleasure working at Sixteenth Century-Fox.   **Jean Renoir**

ADOLPH ZUKOR FILM PRODUCER

Would I comment on Mr. Zukor's visual style? Well, he knew the color of money. No, I didn't say that...   **Peter Bogdanovich**

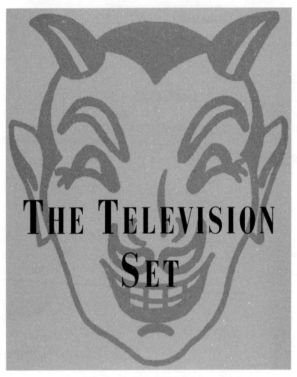

CHAPTER TWO

THE TELEVISION SET

"In California they don't throw their garbage away—they make it into TV shows."

WOODY ALLEN

STEVE ALLEN COMEDIAN

When I can't sleep, I read a book by Steve Allen.   **Oscar Levant**

I'm fond of Steve Allen, but not so much as he is.   **Jack Paar**

LONI ANDERSON ACTRESS

Gravity could be her worst enemy, and she dresses to prove it!
Mr. (Earl) Blackwell

TOM ARNOLD COMEDIAN, ACTOR

My husband and I didn't sign a prenuptual agreement. We signed
a mutual suicide pact.   **Roseanne**

Tom Arnold was a third-rate comedian. Then he married
Roseanne. Great example of a guy who made something of himself, by the sweat of his frau. Or is it the sweat of his sow?

Pinky Lee

Tom Ono.   **Howard Stern**

ED ASNER ACTOR

I don't know him well, but he seems an extremely angry and
short-tempered man. He's enormously sensitive to criticism.

Charlton Heston

ROSEANNE BARR

See *Roseanne*

DIRK BENEDICT ACTOR

You thought Dirk Benedict had problems in TV's "Battlestar
Galactica"? In *Scavenger Hunt*, he really had problems—in one
mercifully brief scene, he was out-acted by a jock strap.

Rona Barrett

JACK BENNY COMEDIAN

I don't want to say that Jack Benny is cheap, but he's got short arms and carries his money low in his pockets. **Fred Allen**

If he can't take it with him, he ain't gonna go.
Eddie "Rochester" Anderson

When Jack Benny has a party, you not only bring your own scotch, you bring your own rocks. **George Burns**

They asked Jack Benny if he would do something for the Actors' Orphanage—so he shot both his parents and moved in.
Bob Hope

There are many things I should like to say about Jack Benny, but I don't believe in biting the ham that feeds you.
Sam Lyons, Benny's agent

MILTON BERLE COMEDIAN

He's done everybody's act. He's a parrot with skin on.
Fred Allen

He's been on TV for years and I finally figured out the reason for his success. He never improved. **Steve Allen**

All I know about television is that I want to get into it as soon as possible—before Milton Berle uses up all my jokes. **Bob Hope**

Berle is responsible for more television sets being sold than anyone else. I sold mine, my father sold his. **Joe E. Lewis**

SANDRA BERNHARD COMEDIENNE

Whether I slept with her or not is irrelevant. I'm perfectly willing to have people think that I did....If it makes people feel better to think that I slept with her, then they can think it. And if it makes them feel safer to think that I didn't, then that's fine too.
Madonna

Sandra used to come on my show a lot before she got a job with that fatso Roseanne and Tom Ono who, because they hate me, have prevented her from coming on my show. **Howard Stern**

CAROL BURNETT COMEDIENNE

Everybody knows I've got bigger boobs than Carol Burnett.

Julie Andrews

GEORGE BURNS COMEDIAN, ACTOR

My husband will never chase another woman. He's too fine, too decent, too old.

Gracie Allen

George reads *Playboy* for the same reason he reads *National Geographic*—to see places he'll never get to visit.

Jackie Gleason

George, you're too old to get married again. Not only can't you cut the mustard, honey, you're too old to open the jar.

LaWanda Page

JOHNNY CARSON "TONIGHT SHOW" HOST

Like, I can't be on none of those television shows 'cause I'd have to tell Johnny Carson, "You're a sad motherfucker." That's the only way I could put it.

Miles Davis

The first time we ever worked together many years ago you were just a snotty guy, and it's nice to know you haven't changed.

Buddy Hackett

It has always been my personal conviction that Carson is the most overrated amateur since Evelyn and her Magic Violin.

Rex Reed

He's an anaesthetist. Prince Valium.

Mort Sahl

LYNDA CARTER ACTRESS, "WONDER WOMAN"

Lynda Carter was just a mannequin—only concerned with the way she looked and the fact that I wouldn't wear the same eye makeup she did.

Debra Winger

DICK CAVETT TELEVISION HOST

Where have you been—living in the subway all your life?

Truman Capote

You speak very good French. In fact, it's so good you could only have learned it in a whorehouse. **Groucho Marx**

You hear it often: Cavett is more intelligent than Johnny Carson and Merv Griffin. It's like saying he's the smartest bear in the zoo. **Mort Sahl**

RICHARD CHAMBERLAIN ACTOR

You're doing it the wrong way 'round, my boy. You're a star and you don't know how to act. **Cedric Hardwicke**

JOAN COLLINS ACTRESS

A hymn to overstatement if there ever was one.
Mr. (Earl) Blackwell

She's common, she can't act—yet she's the hottest female property around these days. If that doesn't tell you something about the state of our industry today, what does? **Stewart Granger**

Everything Joan does is seen as a step towards something that will benefit her. *Everything*. **Bryant Gumbel**

Joan Collins' whole career is a testimony to menopausal chic.
Erica Jong

To the unwashed public she is a star. But to those who know her she's a commodity who would sell her own bowel movement.
Anthony Newley

She looks like she combs her hair with an eggbeater.
Louella Parsons

WALTER CRONKITE NEWSMAN

You can learn more by watching "Let's Make a Deal" than you can by watching Walter Cronkite for a month. **Monty Hall**

PHYLLIS DILLER COMEDIENNE

When she started to play, Steinway came down personally and rubbed his name off the piano. **Bob Hope**

Phyllis Diller's had so many face lifts there's nothing left in her shoes. **Bob Hope**

I treasure every moment that I do not see her.   **Oscar Levant**

We want to congratulate Phyllis Diller on her award. She has just
been named Miss Festering Sore.   **Don Rickles**

Phyllis Diller walked into a psychiatrist's office. The psychiatrist
took one look at her and said, "Get under the couch."

Henny Youngman

SHANNEN DOHERTY ACTRESS

Her friends said it was weird to watch her stand in front of a
judge and say, "I do," because usually when Shannen stands in
front of a judge, she says, "Not guilty."   **Arsenio Hall**

PHIL DONAHUE TALK SHOW HOST

He's the greatest husband in the world, and he's nothing to brag
about.   **Marlo Thomas**

SAM DONALDSON TELEVISION JOURNALIST

The Ayatollah of the White House press corps.   **Ronald Reagan**

MORTON DOWNEY, JR. TALK SHOW HOST

He called me a bleached-blonde idiot and I called him a wart-
faced phony.   **Wally George**

HUGH DOWNS TELEVISION JOURNALIST

If Hugh woke up on Christmas day and found a pile of manure
under the tree, he'd wonder where they were hiding the pony.

Joe Garagiola

FARRAH FAWCETT ACTRESS

The only thing tinier than the bikini Farrah Fawcett wore in
[*Sunburn*] was La Farrah's talent.   **Rona Barrett**

We sat and kissed and kissed until our lips were bloody….It was
unbelievable. She has such a body—that tiny waist, those muscles. I said, "My God, I feel like I'm in bed with Olga Korbut!"

Ryan O'Neal

Maybe it's the hair. Maybe it's the teeth. Maybe it's the intellect. No, it's the hair. **Tom Shales**

DAVID FROST INTERVIEWER, TALK SHOW HOST

I always felt Frost was totally absorbed with himself and had a synthetic personality with a fixed smile carefully adapted to the slick phoniness of ad-agency types, show-business types, and broadcast-executive types. **Howard Cosell**

ZSA ZSA GABOR ACTRESS

As a graduate of the Zsa Zsa Gabor School of Creative Mathematics, I honestly do not know how old I am.

Erma Bombeck

Zsa Zsa The-Bore. Did I spell that right? **Elayne Boosler**

Zsa Zsa Gabor has logged millions of miles just walking up and down wedding aisles. **Phyllis Diller**

She knew more days on which gifts could be given than appear on any holiday calendar. **Conrad Hilton**

You can calculate Zsa Zsa Gabor's age by the rings on her fingers. **Bob Hope**

When Zsa Zsa Gabor went to jail for slapping a cop, the warden put her cellmate on a twenty-four-hour suicide watch. **Jay Leno**

Her face is inscrutable, but I can't vouch for the rest of her.

Oscar Levant

I saw she was one of those blondes who put on ten years if you take a close look at them. **Marilyn Monroe**

I could tell she was attracted to me. I figured we'd go for it and I'd give a little kiss. Her mouth starts to open and now I'm getting nervous, and I'm feeling tongue. There's a lot of fake teeth in that mouth, so I got a little nervous, and I pulled back like a scared schoolgirl. **Howard Stern**

Zsa Zsa Gabor is an expert housekeeper. Every time she gets divorced she keeps the house. **Henny Youngman**

JACKIE GLEASON ACTOR

Jackie cut his finger...it's the first time I ever saw blood with a head on it.

Joey Adams

They call him the Great One; to many of us he's merely the Overweight One.

Betty Grable

Jackie's consistent: he's got a fat mouth and a fat belly.

Joe Namath

MERV GRIFFIN TALK SHOW HOST, ENTERTAINMENT EXECUTIVE

Merv Griffin sings like I look.

Totie Fields

Maybe he lusts after both sexes. Who knows, darling? Frankly, I always thought that Merv was too old and fat to make love at all.

Zsa Zsa Gabor

BUDDY HACKETT COMEDIAN

...a man who willed his body to science, and science is contesting the will.

Red Buttons

ARSENIO HALL TALK SHOW HOST

His head looks like my crotch.

Roseanne

I'm *infinitely* better-looking than Arsenio. He has huge gums and these long, fucked-up fingers. 'Course, he's always telling me I'm fucking ugly.

Eddie Murphy

I met him years ago when he was working for Eddie Murphy. Taking care of his dry cleaning. I should probably take that back.

Charlie Sheen

Assholio...Asskissio.

Howard Stern

BOB HOPE COMEDIAN

Bob Hope is still about as funny as he ever was. I just never thought he was that funny in the first place.

Chevy Chase

How many of his jokes can you recall five minutes after "The Bob Hope Show" goes off the air?

Buster Keaton

Hope is not a comedian. He just translates what others write for him.
Groucho Marx

I think in twenty years I'll be looked at like Bob Hope. Doing those president jokes and golf jokes. It scares me.
Eddie Murphy

GEORGE JESSEL HUMORIST, TELEVISION HOST

As a young boy he was a precocious moron.
Groucho Marx

That son of a bitch started to reminisce when he was eight years old.
Walter Winchell

DON JOHNSON ACTOR

I know Don Johnson and he is scum. He's just a long-haired guy with good looks who makes a bundle selling sex, drugs and violence on commercial television.
Jay Rockefeller

This man is unbearable.
Mickey Rourke

TED KOPPEL TELEVISION JOURNALIST

He's brilliant. I love him. But he does have funny hair.
Steve Allen

MICHAEL LANDON ACTOR

Michael Landon can be a spoiled brat when he wants to be, and he often wants to be.
David Janssen

I did a charity function with Landon once. He was smiley and affable when the camera was on him, but boy, the second it turned off, he didn't have time for anyone except the other VIPs in the room.
Nancy Walker

ROBIN LEACH
TELEVISION PERSONALITY, "LIFESTYLES OF THE RICH AND FAMOUS"

I think I'd probably put a bullet in my head if I had Robin Leach over to my house.
Tim Robbins

DAVID LETTERMAN LATE-NIGHT TALK SHOW HOST

I saw this Letterman once. I didn't think he was funny. He was just being...mildly ironical. **Arthur Miller**

OSCAR LEVANT HUMORIST, PIANIST

A character who, if he did not exist, could not be imagined.
S.N. Behrman

Oscar was a man of principle. He never sponged off anybody he didn't admire. **Harpo Marx**

When Oscar comes on stage he weaves like a drunk trying to find the restroom. He gropes his way to a chair and slumps in it twitching, scowling and clutching his heart. "It might fall out," he once told me. **Jack Paar**

Pearls is a disease of oysters. Levant is a disease of Hollywood.
Kenneth Tynan

There is absolutely nothing wrong with Oscar Levant that a miracle cannot fix. **Alexander Woollcott**

RUSH LIMBAUGH CONSERVATIVE PUNDIT, TALK SHOW HOST

I asked Rush what year he planned on running [for President], and he said, "I couldn't afford the pay cut." **Roger Ailes**

Rush owes me a lot. I feed that big fat head of his.
Howard Stern

JULIA LOUIS-DREYFUSS ACTRESS

It's really astounding to me the variety of things she does well—she's such a *broad* broad. **Jerry Seinfeld**

DENNIS MILLER COMEDIAN, "SATURDAY NIGHT LIVE" ALUMNUS

Dennis is a great stand-up comic but an annoying, arrogant asshole. Amazingly, he switches from a great fun guest one minute to an overly sensitive scumbag the next. **Howard Stern**

RICARDO MONTALBAN ACTOR

Ricardo Montalban is to improvisational acting what Mount Rushmore is to animation.
John Cassavetes

BILL MOYERS TELEVISION JOURNALIST, WRITER, POLITICIAN

Bill Moyers can do a story about a dog taking a leak on a tree and everybody says how eloquent it was. I could do an interview with Jesus Christ and they'd complain I was too soft on him.
Geraldo Rivera

PAT O'BRIEN NEWSCASTER

For slime time it's Pat O'Brien. The late-night anchor is so slick, I can't believe he doesn't slide off his late-night anchor chair. O'Brien is beyond cool; he's cryogenic.
Norman Chad

JACK PAAR ORIGINAL "TONIGHT SHOW" HOST

Paar wanted you to succeed so much that he would help you to the point of tripping you up.
Al Capp

He has a genuine warmth. At the same time he has more reserve and hostility toward an audience than anyone I've ever known. Sometimes I expect him to come out with a whip and a chair.
Hugh Downs

TV's most famous terrorist.
Merv Griffin

MICHAEL PALIN COMEDIAN, "MONTY PYTHON"-ER

Yap, yap, yap he goes, all day long *and* through the night, twenty-three to the dozen, the ground littered with the hind legs of donkey, 'til you believe it is not possible for him to go on any longer, but he *does*.
John Cleese

VICTORIA PRINCIPAL ACTRESS

Victoria Principal has to read a thousand books to become low brow.
Joan Rivers

DON RICKLES COMEDIAN

I like Don Rickles. But that's because I have no taste.

Frank Sinatra

He looks like an extra in a crowd scene by Hieronymus Bosch.

Kenneth Tynan

GERALDO RIVERA TALK SHOW HOST

I'm proud to be living in a free, democratic country like America, where men are men, women are women, and whatever's left is on "Geraldo."　　**Johnny Carson**

He's not the most gorgeous, but you know he would be horrible to you in bed and I like that. Very rough.　　**Zsa Zsa Gabor**

He's such a toad!　　**Bette Midler**

The rest of the people who watch it sit there and think the same thing that you and I think: Geraldo is full of shit.　　**Frank Zappa**

JOAN RIVERS COMEDIENNE, TALK SHOW HOST

Yeah, I eat the same as you. I just don't puke when I'm through.

Roseanne

A depressed area's Don Rickles, only not as pretty.

Roger Moore

ANDY ROONEY TELEVISION CURMUDGEON, "60 MINUTES"

There are best-selling humorists who do get my goat. Andy Rooney springs to mind. Wry. Who needs wry? I haven't got *time* for wry.　　**Roy Blount, Jr.**

ROSEANNE ACTRESS, COMEDIENNE

Roseanne Barr is a bowling ball looking for an alley.

Mr. (Earl) Blackwell

The closest sound to Roseanne Barr's singing the national anthem was my cat being neutered.　　**Johnny Carson**

I watched "Roseanne" once and thought John Goodman stole the show....She's disgusting.　　　　　　　　　　　**Larry Hagman**

The business has been taken over by low-life sluts.　**Bette Midler**

I said [to Tom Arnold],"Listen, buddy, I only *play* the Terminator...you married one."　　　**Arnold Schwarzenegger**

If Roseanne Barr is the new Lucille Ball, I'm the new Garbo.

Nancy Walker

EMMA SAMMS　ACTRESS

We dated in 1984 but I knew going out with a white person wasn't cool careerwise, so I told her we had to eat at McDonald's and keep it low-key.　　　　　　　　　　　**Arsenio Hall**

MARIA SHRIVER　NEWSCASTER

Maria is high maintenance.　　　　**Arnold Schwarzenegger**

TORI SPELLING　ACTRESS, DAUGHTER OF AARON SPELLING

She's really cute, she's on a hit show, and any guy who bags her can back the Brink's truck up to the house.　　**Howard Stern**

HOWARD STERN　"SHOCK" DEEJAY

He could get Mother Teresa to spit on him and walk off the show.

David Brenner

If Howard Stern didn't exist, white trash would not have a super-star.　　　　　　　　　　　　　　　　**Al Sharpton**

ED SULLIVAN　TELEVISION HOST

Ed Sullivan will be around as long as someone else has talent.

Fred Allen

Ed Sullivan has introduced me as Jack Carson, John Crater, John Kerr and Carson McCullers. Now I have my contracts with him made out "To Whom It May Concern."

Jack Carter

While he doesn't sing, dance or tell jokes, he does them equally
well.   **Bing Crosby**

MR. T ACTOR

That buffoon.   **Bryant Gumbel**

MARLO THOMAS ACTRESS

Her face is always suffused with some sort of adorable, tough
wistfulness, a wisecracking yearning; since it is a face that has
clearly undergone intensive restructuring, it may be that the
yearning is that of the remaining parts for those that are gone or
have been shifted around.   **John Simon**

Like a kewpie doll with a bad hairdo and not even cute.

Cornel Wilde

CHARLENE TILTON ACTRESS

A Victorian lampshade holding her breasts. **Mr. (Earl) Blackwell**

BARBARA WALTERS TELEVISION INTERVIEWER

The all-time Olympics award for the dumbest question on TV has
to go to Barbara Walters.   **Jack Paar**

I know how Barbara Walters gets her interview subjects to cry.
She just stays in their house so long, they're so sick of her they
start crying.   **John Tesh**

A hyena in syrup.   **Yevgeny Yevtushenko**

VANNA WHITE LETTER-TURNER, "WHEEL OF FORTUNE"

Mall fashion at its worst.   **Mr. (Earl) Blackwell**

I guess [her] baby's name is Nicholas. She picked Nicholas
because it has five consonants, three vowels, and no letter is
repeated.   **Jay Leno**

OPRAH WINFREY TALK SHOW HOSTESS

I realized in our culture if you don't have a penis, the only true contribution you can make is to lose twenty pounds. Any of your accomplishments pale in comparison. Ask Oprah Winfrey.

Tyne Daly

HENNY YOUNGMAN COMEDIAN

The greatest form of flattery is imitation, and one of Henny's unusual traits is that he is flattered by the fact that for many years he has been an imitation of a comedian. **Milton Berle**

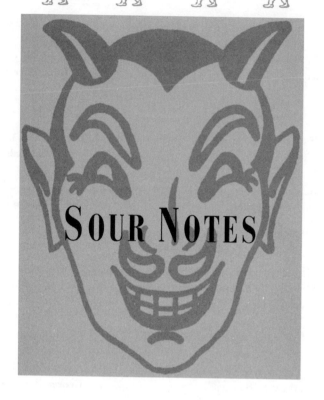

CHAPTER THREE

SOUR NOTES

"I hate music, especially when it's played."

JIMMY DURANTE

FRANKIE AVALON POP SINGER

He was like a prostitute at heart. If you had the right price you had him. **Rona Barrett**

BURT BACHARACH POP SINGER, PIANIST, SONGWRITER

If God had given me Burt Bacharach's persona—the hair, the piano—I would have destroyed the world. **Sammy Cahn**

He called me for a divorce on the phone....He said, "This will only take a minute." **Angie Dickinson**

THE BEATLES POP BAND

They are so unbelievably horrible, so appallingly unmusical, so dogmatically insensitive to the magic of the art, that they qualify as crowned heads of anti-music. **William F. Buckley, Jr.**

...bad-mannered little shits. **Noël Coward**

Having played with other musicians, I don't even think The Beatles were that good. **George Harrison**

I see the Beatles have arrived from England. They were forty pounds overweight, and that was just their hair. **Bob Hope**

I declare that the Beatles are mutants. Prototypes of evolutionary agents sent by God, endowed with a mysterious power to create a new human species—a young race of laughing freemen. **Timothy Leary**

The Beatles never had anything to say. It was always nice, happy stuff. What *did* they ever say? **Lou Reed**

I guess from the outside it seemed like they were the fresh-faced fab mop tops and we [The Rolling Stones] were totally the other end of the spectrum. But they were just as filthy as we were, really. **Keith Richards**

Rock music—it's been a detriment to society from the day it was born. I didn't even like the Beatles. I thought they were little jerks then and I still think they're jerks now.   **George C. Scott**

I rued the day that the Beatles were unfortunately born into this world. They are the people who first made it publicly acceptable to spit in the eye of authority.   **Frank Sinatra, Jr.**

LUDWIG VAN BEETHOVEN COMPOSER

Beethoven's last quartets were written by a deaf man and should only be listened to by a deaf man.   **Thomas Beecham**

What can you do with [the Seventh Symphony]? It's like a lot of yaks jumping about.   **Thomas Beecham**

Having adapted Beethoven's Sixth Symphony for Fantasia, Walt Disney commented, "Gee! This'll make Beethoven."
     Marshall McLuhan

Beethoven always sounds to me like the upsetting of bags of nails, with here and there an also dropped hammer.   **John Ruskin**

I love Beethoven, especially the poems.   **Ringo Starr**

LEONARD BERNSTEIN COMPOSER, CONDUCTOR

Don't ever let him near a microphone.   **Aaron Copland**

He uses music as an accompaniment to his conducting.
     Oscar Levant

CHUCK BERRY ROCK MUSICIAN

Well, now, Chuck Berry was a rock 'n' roll songwriter. So I never tried to write rock 'n' roll songs, 'cause I figured he had just done it.   **Bob Dylan**

I think for the life span he's lasted, Chuck Berry's productivity has been nil, more or less.   **Elton John**

CLINT BLACK COUNTRY SINGER

I find that him being this gorgeous, hunky man, women are understandably aggressive. My male fans are much more shy.
Lisa Hartman

He is the kind of guy a gal would want to take home to meet her father if she could trust her mother.
Buck Owens

JON BON JOVI ROCK SINGER

He's a wimp.
Nikki Sixx

PAT BOONE POP SINGER

I once shook hands with Pat Boone and my whole right side sobered up.
Dean Martin

DAVID BOWIE ROCK SINGER

The nicest fella from Mars I ever met.
Bono

If David Bowie's latest persona is the Thin White Duke, he's going to give a bad name to whites, thin people and peers of the realm.
Freddie Mercury

David Bowie is the most insane-looking human creature I've ever had the misfortune of laying my eyes on.
Frank Sinatra, Jr.

He's a little too fairyish looking for me. I guess it's because I'm American, but I don't like to see boys wearing make-up.
Patti Smith

BOY GEORGE POP SINGER

Boy George is all England needs—another queen who can't dress.
Joan Rivers

JOHANNES BRAHMS COMPOSER

Brahms is just like Tennyson, an extraordinary musician with the brains of a third rate village policeman.
George Bernard Shaw

What a giftless bastard!
Peter Ilyich Tchaikovsky

ANITA BRYANT POP SINGER, ANTI-HOMOSEXUALITY ACTIVIST

While the specter of Chairperson Bryant astride a galloping white horse as a kind of Ginny Orangeseed spreading bigotry throughout the land is certainly theatrical enough, the woman is dangerous.   **Rod McKuen**

WILLIAM BYRD COMPOSER

Byrd's misfortune is that when he is not first-rate he is so rarely second-rate.   **Gustav Holst**

DAVID BYRNE ROCK SINGER, MUSICIAN

He should be the first guy indicted for crimes of such extreme pretension that he's actually physically jailed.

Bob Guccione, Jr.

MARIA CALLAS OPERA SINGER

I will not enter into a public feud with Madame Callas since I am well aware that she has considerably greater competence and experience at that kind of thing than I have.   **Rudolf Bing**

When Callas carried a grudge she planted it, nursed it, fostered it, watered it and watched it grow to sequoia size.

Harold Schonberg

GLEN CAMPBELL COUNTRY/POP SINGER

Granted, he's very popular as he is, and in my opinion one of the finest singers of our time, but he's been exploited. He's also got lousy taste in song material.   **Merle Haggard**

CHARO SINGER, ENTERTAINER

Charo is a one-note song played off-key.   **Ethel Merman**

FRÉDÉRIC CHOPIN COMPOSER

A composer for the right hand.   **Richard Wagner**

PERRY COMO POP SINGER

Perry gave his usual impersonation of a man who has been simultaneously told to say Cheese and shot in the back with a poisoned arrow.
Clive James

I'm convinced that his voice comes out of his eyelids.
Oscar Levant

AARON COPLAND COMPOSER

If a young man of twenty-three can write a symphony like that, in five years he will be ready to commit murder. **Walter Damrosch**

ELVIS COSTELLO ROCK SINGER

They call Elvis Costello four-eyes for a reason. How can you look at him and get off?
Lou Reed

Costello's okay, we played him, but I couldn't call him Elvis.
Tom Petty

BILLY RAY CYRUS COUNTRY SINGER

…not a good singer, but he don't need to be if you look that good.
Waylon Jennings

SAMMY DAVIS. JR. POP SINGER, ENTERTAINER

Forty years ago there was a young Jewish entertainer named Al Jolson who was trying to pass as Negro. Today there is a young Negro entertainer named Sammy Davis who is trying to pass as Jewish.
Goodman Ace

He hits the [golf] ball 130 yards and his jewelry goes 150.
Bob Hope

Sammy Davis, Jr. had his own code of marital fidelity. He explained to me that he could do anything with me except have normal intercourse because that would be cheating on his wife.
Linda Lovelace

I…think Sammy looks better in an African caftan and I wish he'd go back to one. He looks like a headwaiter in a rib joint somewhere.
Frank Sinatra

JOHN DENVER POP SINGER

I'm a John Denver freak. I don't give a shit that he looks like a fucking turkey.   **Grace Slick**

DEVO "NEW WAVE" GROUP

It's nice to see an act whose audience can't relate to them.

Leonard Cohen

HOWARD DIETZ THEATRICAL LYRICIST

I understand your new play is full of single entendres.

George S. Kaufman

FATS DOMINO ROCK MUSICIAN

I remember when I was very young—this is very serious—I read an article by Fats Domino which has really influenced me. He said, "You should never sing the lyrics out very clearly."

Mick Jagger

THE DOORS ROCK GROUP

I tried marijuana one time but it didn't do anything for me 'cept give me a headache. Sheeet, I played a gig with the Doors once and those boys smoked so much of that stuff you could get a headache just walkin' into their dressin' room.   **Glen Campbell**

BOB DYLAN ROCK/FOLK SINGER

I've already forgotten who Bob Dylan was.   **Elvis Costello**

Dylan once said to Keith [Richards], "I could have written 'Satisfaction' but you couldn't have written 'Tambourine Man'."

Mick Jagger

FABIAN POP SINGER, TEEN SENSATION

I am 39 and already I can't relate to Fabian.   **Lenny Bruce**

ARETHA FRANKLIN SOUL SINGER

They asked me what I thought of black power. I said black power is me making it with Aretha Franklin. **Junior Wells**

GEORGE GERSHWIN COMPOSER

Tell me, George, if you had to do it over would you fall in love with yourself again? **Oscar Levant**

EYDIE GORME POP SINGER

There really isn't a Steve Lawrence, you know. Eydie's a ventriloquist. **Steve Lawrence**

GEORGE FRIDERIC HANDEL COMPOSER

A tub of pork and beer. **Hector Berlioz**

GEORGE HARRISON FORMER BEATLE

In his book, which is purportedly this clarity of vision of each song he wrote and its influences, he remembers every two-bit sax player or guitarist he met in subsequent years. I'm not in the book. **John Lennon**

If you see George Harrison you can tell him I think he's a load of old rope. **Cliff Richard**

JOSEPH HAYDN COMPOSER

So far as genius can exist in a man who is merely virtuous, Haydn had it. He went as far as the limits that morality sets to intellect. **Friedrich Nietzsche**

JIMI HENDRIX ROCK SINGER, GUITARIST

I think I can put together a better rock band than Jimi Hendrix. **Miles Davis**

I first heard Hendrix when I was driving my mother's station wagon in New Hampshire. There aren't too many radio stations there—you just got bits and pieces through the static. I heard "Purple Haze" and I thought, "Now we're getting Martian radio."

Joe Perry

ENGELBERT HUMPERDINCK POP SINGER

He was a doll and a gentleman, but his pants were so tight he couldn't move. I used to tease him by saying, "You know, your buns are supposed to move separately!"

Chita Rivera

BILLY IDOL ROCK SINGER

The Perry Como of punk.

John Lydon (Johnny Rotten)

MICHAEL JACKSON POP STAR

Where else but in America can a poor black boy like Michael Jackson grow up to be a rich white woman?

Red Buttons

Now Michael Jackson says his skin turned white by itself. What about his nose, his lips and his hair? Did they also decide to turn Caucasian by themselves?

Boy George

We call Michael Jackson "Smelly" because he's so polite and proper we can't even get him to say the word *funky*.

Quincy Jones

He's a very strange person.

Stephen King

Apparently, Michael Jackson really has married Elvis Presley's daughter. It sounds like a National Enquirer story, but there are witnesses—a space alien, a dog-faced boy and a 120-pound baby.

Conan O'Brien

He is the least weird man I've ever known.

Elizabeth Taylor

MICK JAGGER ROCK SINGER

I think Mick Jagger would be astounded and amazed if he realized to how many people he is not a sex symbol but a mother image.

David Bowie

He's a fossil. His wife can keep him. **Carla Bruni**

He moves like a parody between a majorette girl and Fred Astaire.
Truman Capote

He's stoned on himself. He's always in complete control and the whole thing is manipulation. It really bothers me that a twerp like that can parade around and convince everybody that he's Satan.
Ry Cooder

That cunt is a great entertainer. **Bill Graham**

He sees all women as tarts. **Bianca Jagger**

I know people theorize that Mick thought it would be amusing to marry his twin. But actually he wanted to achieve the ultimate by making love to himself. **Bianca Jagger**

I think Mick's a joke, with all that fag dancing; I always did.
John Lennon

From when I first met him, I saw Mick was in love with Keith [Richards]. It still is that way. **Anita Pallenberg**

I'm his friend and he knows it. It's just like, "I love you, darling, but I can't live with you." **Keith Richards**

Can't open a paper now without seeing a picture of him at some film opening cooing into Baryshnikov's ear....I mean, the First Lady of Canada starts hanging out with him and she's accused of social climbing. **Garry Trudeau**

He stole my music but he gave me my name. **Muddy Waters**

I really just put any old thing on. Not like Mick, with his fabrics and colors. He's like fucking Greta Garbo. **Charlie Watts**

JOAN JETT ROCK SINGER

Why do all heavy metal guitarists look like Joan Jett?
Boy George

ELTON JOHN FLAMBOYANT ROCK SINGER/MUSICIAN

I don't think he was ever born to be a rock 'n' roll star. He was probably born to be chairman of Watford Football Club and now he's beginning to look like the Chairman of Watford Football Club, as well. **Rod Stewart**

GEORGE JONES COUNTRY SINGER

The first time I met George Jones he was in bed with another woman. **Tammy Wynette**

RICKIE LEE JONES POP SINGER

Her style onstage was appealing and arousing, sort of like that of a sexy white spade. **Tom Waits**

TOM JONES POP SINGER

Tom Jones's pants are so tight they wear out on the inside.
Joey Adams

CAROLE KING POP SINGER

Once in a while when I turn on the radio in the car, the lyrics I hear are really banal. Toast—when I hear Carole King, I think of toast. **Paul Simon**

KRIS KRISTOFFERSON SINGER, ACTOR

Kris always wanted me to sing his demos—and with good reason.
Mel Tillis

FRANKIE LAINE POP SINGER

...a beefy man with a strangler's hands and a smile like the beam of a lighthouse, but he sings almost exclusively about tears and regrets. You form a mental picture of him sobbing into his pillow, hammering it with his fists until the bed collapses under him.
Kenneth Tynan

JOHN LENNON ROCK SINGER, SONGWRITER, MUSICIAN

He could be a maneuvering swine, which no one ever realized.

Paul McCartney

If you want to hear pretentiousness, just listen to John Lennon's "Imagine." All that "possessions" crap.

Lou Reed

John Lennon ain't no revolutionary—he's a fucking idiot.

Todd Rundgren

LIBERACE PIANIST, SHOWMAN

Such dimpling and winking! Such tossing of blond curls and fluttering of eyelashes and flashing of teeth! Such nausea.

Faye Emerson

MADONNA POP SINGER, SOMETIME ACTRESS

She's jumped right into the movie game…but I think people should learn to act first, you know what I mean? **Rosanna Arquette**

Madonna's got one big choice. Take a couple of years off and become a human being. **Sandra Bernhard**

It would be my guess that Madonna is not a very happy woman. From my own experience, having gone through persona changes like that, that kind of clawing need to be the center of attention is not a pleasant place to be. **David Bowie**

I read this thing that says she's a genius at selling sex. That really takes a lot of genius! I think we should start an organization like Rock the Vote, which she advertised in her underwear. I want to start an organization called Gag the Hussy. **Elvis Costello**

She's not only a terrifyingly bad actress, she barely seems like a human being. **David Denby**

Sometimes you feel like a tamer with a she-lion in a cage. You have to force her to jump through this burning hoop, and there are just two possibilities. Either she'll jump through the ring of fire…or she'll kill you. **Uli Edel**

I don't think Madonna can really do much more to shock anybody unless she becomes a nun.   **Janet Jackson**

She wears enough costumes every other day of the year; Halloween is like her day off.   **Alek Keshishian**

Marketing is something I'm very proud of. The only artist that does it better than me is Madonna. She's the champ.   **Spike Lee**

She is closer to organized prostitution than anything else.

Morrissey

I'd never kissed anybody onscreen and I came clean with her....She taught me how to do the kissing, and then she joked, "If you slip me the tongue I'll kill you."   **Mike Myers**

It was all rumor. I never met the woman.   **Sean Penn**

She is so hairy...when she lifted up her arm, I thought it was Tina Turner in her armpit.   **Joan Rivers**

As for ambition, she makes Streisand look squishy.   **Liz Smith**

If there's a mountain called Egomania, she finally climbed to the top of it with that piece of garbage [*Truth or Dare*].

Howard Stern

Madonna—she's like toilet paper. She's on every magazine cover in the world. Devalued.   **Oliver Stone**

I could rip her throat out. I can sing better than she can, if that counts for anything.   **Meryl Streep**

She's like a breast with a boom box.   **Judy Tenuta**

One copy of her book [*Sex*] is probably the most instant turnoff that anybody could see.   **Andrew Lloyd Webber**

BARRY MANILOW POP SINGER, MUSICIAN

Barry Manilow looks like you do when you see your face in the reflection of a bathroom faucet.   **Curt Marsh**

PAUL McCARTNEY ROCK SINGER, MUSICIAN

Paul's really writing for a fourteen-year-old audience now.

George Harrison

I'd join a band with John Lennon any day, but I wouldn't join a band with Paul McCartney.

George Harrison

GEORGE MICHAEL POP SINGER

I'll wear anything as long as it hasn't been on George Michael's back.

Boy George

Come on, George. Loosen up. Swing, man. And no more of that talk about "the tragedy of fame." The tragedy of fame is when no one shows up and you're singing to the cleaning lady in some empty joint that hasn't seen a paying customer since St. Swithin's Day.

Frank Sinatra

ROGER MILLER POP SINGER

He thinks it's funny to call people on his portable phone from just outside their motel room doors, then knock. **Merle Haggard**

JONI MITCHELL POP/FOLK SINGER

Joni Mitchell is about as modest as Mussolini.

David Crosby

Joni Mitchell is almost like a *man*.

Bob Dylan

JIM MORRISON ROCK SINGER, POET

I like to think of us [The Velvet Underground] as Clearasil on the face of the nation. Jim Morrison would have said that if he was smart, but he's dead.

Lou Reed

The path of excess leads to a dirt plot in a foreign land that people pour booze on and put out cigarettes on.

Axl Rose

The idiot drowned in a bathtub. Is that cool? I don't think so. It's a lot harder to stay alive and deal with it. And he couldn't even sing for shit.

Joe Walsh

WOLFGANG AMADEUS MOZART COMPOSER

Ah Mozart! He was happily married—but his wife wasn't.

Victor Borge

It is sobering to consider that when Mozart was my age he had already been dead for a year.

Tom Lehrer

There's shit on [my] record Mozart wishes he could have thought of.

Ted Nugent

The sonatas of Mozart are unique; they are too easy for children and too difficult for artists.

Artur Schnabel

WILLIE NELSON COUNTRY SINGER, MUSICIAN

Down in Texas they think that when they die they go to Willie's house.

Waylon Jennings

It is not officially summer until Willie Nelson puts his hair up in a red bandanna.

David Letterman

Q: What has 300 legs and seven teeth? A: The front row at a Willie Nelson concert.

***Playboy* magazine**

RANDY NEWMAN POP SINGER, SONGWRITER

His mouth turns down at the corners and he doesn't have any lips—sort of like you would imagine Oscar Wilde if he were a trout.

Charles M. Young

JOHN OATES POP SINGER/MUSICIAN, HALL & OATES

Men don't particularly turn me on. And no, John and I have never been lovers. He's not my type. Too short and dark.

Daryl Hall

YOKO ONO POP SINGER

She doesn't suffer fools gladly, even if she's married to him.

John Lennon

Her voice sounded like an eagle being goosed.

Ralph Novak

If I found her floating in my pool, I'd punish my dog.

Joan Rivers

OZZY OSBOURNE HEAVY METAL SINGER

Ozzy Osbourne is a moron. He couldn't carry a tune around in a suitcase.   **Ronnie James Dio**

MARIE OSMOND POP SINGER

Marie Osmond makes Mother Teresa look like a slut.

Joan Rivers

DOLLY PARTON COUNTRY SINGER

I have nothing against the gal, but I'll bet most of her fans are either hillbillies or diabetics.   **Peter Allen**

Too many yards of Dolly poured into too few yards of fabric.

Mr. (Earl) Blackwell

As a football player at Princeton I always felt like Dolly Parton's shoulder straps—I knew I had a job to do but I felt totally incapable of doing it.   **James Stewart**

PETER, PAUL & MARY FOLK GROUP

If I had a hammer I'd use it on Peter, Paul and Mary.

Howard Rosenberg

COLE PORTER COMPOSER

He sang like a hinge.   **Ethel Merman**

ELVIS PRESLEY ROCK SINGER, ACTOR

He's an animal. Definitely an animal. A very interesting animal.

Ann-Margret

Elvis Presley wound up looking on the outside what he always was on the inside—an overrated slob.   **Joan Blondell**

There's a tendency for people to mythologize everybody [as] evil or good. Elvis Presley—bloated, over the hill, adolescent entertainer suddenly drawing people to Las Vegas—has nothing to do with excellence, just myth. **Marlon Brando**

If life was fair, Elvis would be alive and all the impersonators would be dead. **Johnny Carson**

One critic wrote, "I've found somebody to replace Tony Curtis as the world's worst actor—Elvis Presley." **Tony Curtis**

He might possibly be classified as an entertainer. Or perhaps quite as easily as an assignment for a sociologist. **Jack Gould**

When I first knew Elvis he had a million dollars worth of talent. Now he has a million dollars. **Colonel Tom Parker**

Elvis was the kind of white trash-turned-star that, when the Beatles came along, he called them sissies or Communists because they knocked him right out of the limelight. **Johnnie Ray**

THE ARTIST FORMERLY KNOWN AS PRINCE POP SINGER

He's terribly demanding and expects women to know their place. He was always far too busy for a genuine affair to develop. I suspect he looked at me as a potential business prospect more than anything else. **Kim Basinger**

A toothpick wrapped in a purple doilie! **Mr. (Earl) Blackwell**

He's sleeping with all these gorgeous white women and never talking about it himself but getting *them* to talk about it and ruin their careers in the South. **Carrie Fisher**

Prince looks like a dwarf who's been dipped in a bucket of pubic hair. **Boy George**

I talked to Prince on the phone once after he got two cans thrown at him in L.A. He said he didn't want to do any more shows. God, I got *thousands* of bottles and cans thrown at me. Every kind of debris. **Mick Jagger**

LOU RAWLS SOUL SINGER

Don't you think we could have a beautiful chocolate-colored daughter together? **Margaret Trudeau**

HELEN REDDY POP SINGER

She doesn't know who she is. She wears see-through clothes that show her bosoms—whatever they are. **Mr. (Earl) Blackwell**

They arrested Helen Reddy for loitering in front of an orchestra. **Bette Midler**

KEITH RICHARDS GUITARIST, THE ROLLING STONES

I wouldn't piss on him if he were on fire. **Sid Vicious**

He's the only dirty man I know who doesn't smell. **Ron Wood**

LIONEL RICHIE POP SINGER

I learned to be cheap from Lionel Richie, who is the cheapest person in the world. **Bette Midler**

AXL ROSE ROCK SINGER, GUNS N' ROSES

If I was as ugly as Axl Rose I'd be pissed off about cameras going off in my face, too. **Ted Nugent**

Axl is fucking pissed off and angry, I want you to know. There's a deep, dark well of Axl. The public doesn't know half about this fucking guy. **Steven Tyler**

JOHNNY ROTTEN (JOHN LYDON) PUNK SINGER

I can imagine him becoming a successful hairdresser, a singing Vidal Sassoon. **Malcolm McLaren**

ARNOLD SCHOENBERG COMPOSER

He'd be better off shoveling snow. **Richard Strauss**

THE SEX PISTOLS PIONEERING PUNK BAND

It seems to me that it was with the Pistols that rock's luck finally ran out.
Stephen King

DINAH SHORE POP SINGER, ENTERTAINER

I never watch the Dinah Shore show—I'm a diabetic.
Oscar Levant

FRANK SINATRA SINGER, ACTOR

I'm just one of those who thought they could *direct* Sinatra. It's like being one of the girls who thought they'd get Howard Hughes to marry them.
Robert Aldrich

He has about as much humor as this floor.
Lauren Bacall

He's the kind of guy that when he dies he's going up to heaven and give God a bad time for making him bald.
Marlon Brando

Talk about heart, he's it. Here's a man who last Christmas gave Sammy Davis, Jr. a half-bottle of Murine.
Red Buttons

I was not impressed by the creeps and Mafia types he kept about him.
Prince Charles

Frank gets picked on by people who want to see how tough he is and he usually obliges them with a demonstration.
Bing Crosby

When Frank Sinatra was down he was sweet, but when he got back up he was hell.
Ava Gardner

When he dies, they're giving his zipper to the Smithsonian.
Dean Martin

I've stayed in his house and he has bored me to death. He tells the sa-a-ame stories he's been telling for years, and all I ever heard were his records, which he played *over* and *over* again.
Phyllis McGuire

Make yourself at home, Frank. Hit somebody.
Don Rickles

You're off-key, your voice is shot. Stop singing. You annoy people.
Don Rickles

I think he's an ill-bred swine who operates on the level of an animal.
David Susskind

Please, God, don't let us be near when his mood changes, when plates and tables fly through the air, when strong men cower and cringe, and when everybody takes to the cyclone cellars.
Earl Wilson

GRACE SLICK ROCK SINGER

She is like somebody's mom who'd a few too many drinks at a cocktail party.
Nick Lowe

PATTI SMITH ROCK SINGER

She wouldn't be bad looking if she would wash up and glue herself together a little better.
Andy Warhol

SONNY & CHER POP SINGERS, ENTERTAINERS

Sonny and Cher are a drag. A guy gets kicked out of a restaurant and he went home and wrote a song about it.
Bob Dylan

SPANDAU BALLET ROCK GROUP

Even if Spandau Ballet were to become great at what it does, what it does would still be the most cretinous sort of Anglo-Yuppie muzak imaginable.
Kurt Loder

You can't drink on an eight-hour flight, pass out and then go on stage....Well, you can, but then you're Spandau Ballet.
Robert Smith

BRUCE SPRINGSTEEN ROCK SINGER, MUSICIAN, SONGWRITER

We used to eat guys like him for breakfast.
Patti Smith

ROD STEWART ROCK SINGER

Rod Stewart is a dangerous person as far as I'm concerned, if you're a woman. Because even if you go out with him once it's plastered everywhere, and for some fucking weird reason he's always used it as a method of getting attention. He gets something from being with anybody who's a little bit in the public eye....He was just a guy, a little jerk.   **Bebe Buell**

Soddy was my pet name for Rod. There were times when he was such a sod even in his most charming moods.   **Britt Ekland**

STING ROCK SINGER

Somebody should clip Sting around the head and tell him to stop singing in that ridiculous Jamaican accent.   **Elvis Costello**

Sting was boring and pretentious. Everyone was driven to distraction by his endless speeches on political matters.

Kathleen Turner

RICHARD STRAUSS COMPOSER

Such an astounding lack of talent was never before united to such pretentiousness.   **Peter Ilyich Tchaikovsky**

IGOR STRAVINSKY COMPOSER

His music used to be original. Now it is aboriginal.

Ernest Newman

BARBRA STREISAND POP SINGER, ACTRESS

Ringo Starr in drag.   **Mr. (Earl) Blackwell**

When she's 'kvetching' I simply say: "Shut up and give me a little kiss, will ya, huh?", or "Stick out your boobs, they're beautiful." And after that she's fine for the next ten minutes.

Peter Bogdanovich

...those grotesque little finger-extensions like Freddy Krueger or Ming the Merciless.   **Georgia Brown**

She takes every ballad and turns it into a three-act opera.

Truman Capote

Barbra Streisand's a *dawg*...[she's] got long fingernails and a good voice, but her *face!* It looks as though a truck ran into it.

Divine

Barbra Streisand overwhelms her material with vocal pyrotechnics.

Michael Feinstein

She scares me to death.

Marvin Hamlisch

She really ought to be called Barbra Strident. **Stanley Kauffman**

She has outdone me. Could I have greeted Slobodan Milosevic by saying, "Hello, Gorgeous"? Could I have flicked my perfectly manicured fingernails at his temples and said, "In my country, powerful men seldom have such thick hair"? I think not.

Henry Kissinger

I'm Number Ten [at the box office]. Right under Barbra Streisand. Can you imagine being *under* Barbra Streisand? Get me a bag—I may throw up.

Walter Matthau

I would be willing to work with her again—on a more equitable level.

Jack Nicholson

We are dining tonight at the Russian Tea Room. Hope to catch a glimpse of Barbra Streisand or Karl Malden or anyone else with a slightly odd nose.

Michael Palin

She's got the balls of a Russian infantryman.

Martin Ritt

The difficulty is that even when Miss Streisand labors to appear sensitive and vulnerable, she cannot conquer our impression that, were she to collide with a Mack truck, it is the truck that would drop dead.

John Simon

DONNA SUMMER DISCO SINGER

I'm not saying this to be cool, but disco sucks—I mean, can you imagine some kid wanting to grow up and play on a Donna Summer album?

Lou Reed

RENATA TEBALDI OPERA SINGER

She had dimples of iron. **Rudolf Bing**

ARTURO TOSCANINI CONDUCTOR

A glorified bandmaster! **Thomas Beecham**

IKE TURNER ROCK MUSICIAN

Ike was like a king. When he woke up I'd have to do his hair, do his nails, his feet....I was a little slave girl. **Tina Turner**

TINA TURNER ROCK SINGER

She told me how all those moves that look so wild and rough are actually meticulously planned. Sexuality wasn't shoved in the audience's face. Her pelvis always moved side to side, not back to front. **Angela Bassett**

STEVEN TYLER ROCK SINGER, AEROSMITH

To be the kind of lead singer that he is—it takes a weird animal to do that shit. **Joe Perry**

VANILLA ICE RAPPER

He says he's street. He ain't from no street. What street's he from, Sesame Street? **Ice-T**

STEVIE RAY VAUGHN ROCK GUITARIST

Stevie Ray's a trip. I've never seen anybody attack a guitar like he does. He plays so loud that, I mean, I was in fear of not being able to have children. **Don Johnson**

SID VICIOUS PUNK MUSICIAN

Sid Vicious died for what? So that we might rock? I mean, it's garbage, you know? **John Lennon**

RICHARD WAGNER COMPOSER

I love Wagner, but the music I prefer is that of a cat hung up by its tail outside a window and trying to stick to the panes of glass with its claws.   **Charles Baudelaire**

Wagner, thank the fates, is no hypocrite. He says out what he means, and he usually means something nasty.   **James Huneker**

This is not music....It is a perfumed fog, shot through with lightning! It is the end of all honesty in art.   **Thomas Mann**

Is Wagner a human being at all? Is he not rather a disease? Everything he touches falls ill. He has made music sick.
Friedrich Nietzsche

Wagner has beautiful moments but awful quarter-hours.
Gioacchino Antonio Rossini

Wagner's music is better than it sounds.   **Mark Twain**

I am quick to agree with Nietzsche that the thundering, melodious balderdash of Wagner was the most addling experience imaginable for the German intellect.   **Kurt Vonnegut, Jr.**

I like Wagner's music better than anybody's. It's so loud that one can talk the whole time without other people hearing what one says.   **Oscar Wilde**

DIONNE WARWICK POP SINGER

Dionne Warwick says she is moving to Brazil. She says that last [Los Angeles] earthquake really got to her and she is fed up. Now, of all people, shouldn't she have known that this earthquake was coming? Those stupid psychic friends of hers.
Jay Leno

CHARLIE WATTS DRUMMER, THE ROLLING STONES

Don't believe him when he says he only joined [The Rolling Stones] on a temporary basis, ha-ha. It was the only gig he could get.   **Mick Jagger**

SOUR NOTES | 109

ANDREW LLOYD WEBBER THEATRICAL COMPOSER

Andrew Lloyd Webber is gobshit. I wouldn't do anything he's
associated with.   **Roland Gift**

LAWRENCE WELK BANDLEADER, ENTERTAINER

Lawrence was not known as the hippest show around. But when
nobody was home, I'd tune in.   **Gregory Hines**

BRIAN WILSON POP MUSICIAN, THE BEACH BOYS

I thought Brian was a perfect gentleman, apart from buttering his
head and trying to put it between two slices of bread.   **Tom Petty**

FRANK ZAPPA ROCK MUSICIAN, SINGER

You're not as ugly as you look in your pictures.   **John Lennon**

I enjoyed those shows I did in London at The Rainbow....I kept
thinking, Frank Zappa fell seventeen feet down into that pit. I
hate Frank Zappa, and it made me so happy to think about that.
Lou Reed

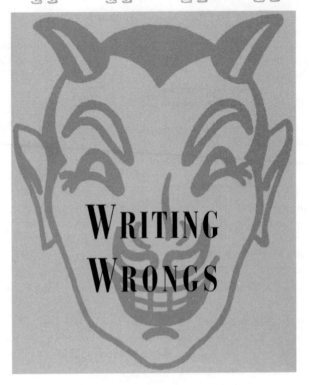

Writing Wrongs

"Writers are a little below clowns
and a little above trained seals."

John Steinbeck

EDWARD ALBEE PLAYWRIGHT

Edward Albee is a wonderful plagiarist. He has wonderful taste in the people he steals from, mainly Strindberg.   **Geraldine Page**

ARISTOPHANES PLAYWRIGHT

The language of Aristophanes reeks of his miserable quackery...his arrogance is insufferable and all honest men detest his malice.   **Plutarch**

MATTHEW ARNOLD POET, CRITIC

I met Matthew Arnold and had a few words with him. He is not as handsome as his photographs—or his poetry.   **Henry James**

Poor Matt, he's gone to heaven, no doubt—but he won't like God.   **Robert Louis Stevenson**

ISAAC ASIMOV PROLIFIC SCI-FI WRITER

Why aren't you at home writing a book?   **Alan Alda**

Isaac Asimov turned into a dirty old man at the age of fifteen.
                                                                                    Frederick Pohl

LOUIS AUCHINCLOSS LAWYER, AUTHOR

He's a second-rate Stephen Birmingham. And Stephen Birmingham is third-rate.   **Truman Capote**

W.H. AUDEN POET, PLAYWRIGHT

Wystan doesn't love God, he's just attracted to him.
                                                                                    Marc Blitzstein

He is all ice and woodenfaced acrobatics.   **Wyndham Lewis**

A high watermark, so to speak, of socialist literature is W.H. Auden, a sort of gutless Kipling.   **George Orwell**

JEAN M. AUEL HISTORICAL NOVELIST

The reason for the success of *Clan of the Cave Bear* is that it's about a Cro-Magnon child being raised by a family of Neanderthals—a position almost all of us have been in.

Lawrence Block

JANE AUSTEN NOVELIST

I am at a loss to understand why people hold Miss Austen's novels at so high a rate....Never was life so pinched and narrow.

Ralph Waldo Emerson

Jane Austen's books too are absent from this library. Just that one omission alone would make a fairly good library out of a library that hadn't a book in it.

Mark Twain

J.M. BARRIE NOVELIST, PLAYWRIGHT, *PETER PAN*

A triumph of sugar over diabetes.

George Jean Nathan

MAX BEERBOHM NOVELIST, ESSAYIST

He is a shallow, affected, self-conscious fribble.

Vita Sackville-West

He has the most remarkable and seductive genius—and I should say about the smallest in the world.

Lytton Strachey

Tell me, when you are alone with Max, does he take off his face and reveal his mask?

Oscar Wilde

ROBERT BENCHLEY DRAMA CRITIC, ESSAYIST, HUMORIST

Robert Benchley has a style that is weak and lies down frequently to rest.

Max Eastman

An enchanting toad of a man.

Helen Hayes

ARNOLD BENNETT NOVELIST, JOURNALIST, PLAYWRIGHT

The Hitler of the book racket.

Wyndham Lewis

Whatever his interest in good writing, he never showed the public anything but his AVARICE. Consequently they adored him.

Ezra Pound

AMBROSE BIERCE POET, JOURNALIST, SHORT STORY WRITER

Born in a log cabin, Ambrose Bierce defied Alger's Law and did not become president.

Clifton Fadiman

Bierce would bury his best friend with a sigh of relief and express satisfaction that he was done with him.

Jack London

WILLIAM BLAKE POET, ARTIST, MYSTIC

There was nothing of the superior person about him. This makes him terrifying.

T.S. Eliot

There is no doubt that this poor man was mad, but there is something in the madness of this man which interests me more than the sanity of Lord Byron and Walter Scott. **William Wordsworth**

BERTOLT BRECHT POET, PLAYWRIGHT

Brecht has not only never had an original thought, he takes twice as long as the average playgoer to have any thought at all.

Robert Morley

HEYWOOD BROUN JOURNALIST

Heywood Broun and I had one thing in common: he was fired from as many newspapers as I have been fired out of political parties.

Fiorello La Guardia

Any mouse can make this elephant squeal. **Alexander Woollcott**

ELIZABETH BARRETT BROWNING POET

Fate has not been kind to Mrs. Browning. Nobody reads her, nobody discusses her, nobody troubles to put her in her place.
Virginia Woolf

ROBERT BROWNING POET

I don't think Browning was very good in bed....He snored and had fantasies about twelve-year-old girls. **W.H. Auden**

Old Hippety-Hop o' the accents **Ezra Pound**

He floods acres of paper with brackets and inverted commas.
Robert Louis Stevenson

He has plenty of music in him but he cannot get it out.
Alfred, Lord Tennyson

ROBERT AND ELIZABETH BARRETT BROWNING
POETS, SPOUSES

Well, I hope they understand one another—nobody else would.
William Wordsworth

EDWARD BULWER-LYTTON NOVELIST, PLAYWRIGHT

He never wrote an invitation to dinner without an eye to posterity. **Benjamin Disraeli**

He is the very pimple of the age's humbug.
Nathaniel Hawthorne

LORD BYRON POET

He seems to me the most *vulgar-minded* genius that ever produced a great effect in literature. **George Eliot**

Mad, bad, and dangerous to know. **Lady Caroline Lamb**

The aristocratic rebel, since he has enough to eat, must have other causes of discontent. **Bertrand Russell**

The most affected of sensualists and the most pretentious of profligates. **Algernon Swinburne**

There is no believing a word they say—your professional poets, I mean—there never existed a more worthless set than Byron and his friends, for example. **Arthur Wellesley, Duke of Wellington**

Lord Byron has spoken severely of my compositions. However faulty they may be, I do not think that I ever could have prevailed upon myself to print such lines as he has done. **William Wordsworth**

JAMES M. CAIN "POTBOILER" NOVELIST

Everything he writes smells like a billy goat. **Raymond Chandler**

TRUMAN CAPOTE NOVELIST, SHORT STORY WRITER, GOSSIP

I've done as much for golf as Truman Capote has for sumo wrestling. **Bob Hope**

Say anything you want about me, but you make fun of my picture and you'll regret it the rest of your fat midget life. **Joshua Logan**

Never gossip about people you don't know. This deprives simple artisans like Truman Capote of work. **P.J. O'Rourke**

He'd be all right if he took his finger out of his mouth. **Harold Robbins**

For God's sake! What's that? **Harold Ross**

Every generation gets the Tiny Tim that it deserves. **Gore Vidal**

I always said little Truman had a voice so high it could only be detected by a bat. **Tennessee Williams**

THOMAS CARLYLE HISTORIAN, AUTHOR

It was very good of God to let Carlyle and Mrs. Carlyle marry one another and so make only two people miserable instead of four.
Samuel Butler

Carlyle has led us all out into the desert and he has left us there.
A.H. Clough

We smile at his clotted English. **Oliver Wendell Holmes**

The same old sausage, fizzing and sputtering in its own grease.
Henry James

He had a daily secretion of curses which he had to vent on somebody or something. **Herbert Spencer**

BENNETT CERF JOURNALIST, EDITOR, PUBLISHER, AUTHOR

I've always told you, Bennett, you're a very nice boy but you're rather stupid. **Gertrude Stein**

GEOFFREY CHAUCER POET

And Chaucer, with his infantine
Familiar clasp of things divine;
That mark upon his lip is wine. **Elizabeth Barrett Browning**

Mr. C. had talent, but he couldn't spel. No man has a right to be a lit'rary man onless he knows how to spel. It is a pity that Chawcer, who had geneyus, was so unedicated. He's the wus speller I know of. **Artemus Ward**

G.K. CHESTERTON POET, ESSAYIST, MYSTERY NOVELIST

Chesterton is like a vile scum on a pond. **Ezra Pound**

TOM CLANCY NOVELIST, "TECHNO-THRILLERS"

Tom Clancy's macho novels are not meant so much for men as overgrown boys. The sexiest items in his novels are the pieces of military hardware, which are unfailingly described in loving, sensuous detail. **Mordechai Richler**

SAMUEL TAYLOR COLERIDGE POET, ESSAYIST, CRITIC

Never did I see such apparatus got ready for thinking, and so little thought. He mounts scaffolding, pulleys and tackle, gathers all the tools in the neighborhood with labor, with noise, demonstration, precept, abuse, and sets—three bricks. **Thomas Carlyle**

The round-faced man in black entered, and dissipated all doubts on the subject by beginning to talk. He did not cease while he stayed; nor has he since, that I know of. **William Hazlitt**

CYRIL CONNOLLY NOVELIST, ESSAYIST, CRITIC

Writers like Connolly gave pleasure a bad name. **E.M. Forster**

JOSEPH CONRAD NOVELIST

Conrad spent a day finding the *mot juste* and then killed it.
Ford Madox Ford

JAMES FENIMORE COOPER NOVELIST

Every time a Cooper person is in peril and absolute silence is worth four dollars a minute, he is sure to step on a dry twig. There may be a hundred handier things to step on, but that wouldn't satisfy Cooper. Cooper requires him to turn out and find a dry twig; and if he can't do it, go and borrow one.
Mark Twain

NOËL COWARD PLAYWRIGHT, ACTOR

Noël and I were in Paris once. Adjoining rooms, of course. One night I felt mischievous, so I knocked on Noël's door and he asked, "Who is it?" I lowered my voice and said, "Hotel detective. Have you got a gentleman in your room?" He answered, "Just a minute, I'll ask him." **Beatrice Lillie**

It's only people who are hysterical who can play hysterical parts. **Sybil Thorndike**

Coward invented the concept of cool. And if his face suggested an old boot, it was unquestionably hand-made. **Kenneth Tynan**

Destiny's tot. **Alexander Woollcott**

STEPHEN CRANE NOVELIST, SHORT STORY WRITER, POET

I had thought that there could be only two worse writers than Stephen Crane, namely two Stephen Cranes. **Ambrose Bierce**

E.E. CUMMINGS POET, PAINTER

His mind was essentially extemporaneous. His fits of poetic fury were like the maenadic seizures described in Greek lyrics. **John Dos Passos**

One imagines him giving off poems as spontaneously as perspiration and with as little application of the intellect. **Edmund Wilson**

DANTE (DANTE ALIGHIERI) POET

A hyena that wrote poetry in tombs. **Friedrich Nietzsche**

All right, then, I'll say it. Dante makes me sick. **Lope de Vega**

DANIEL DEFOE NOVELIST, *ROBINSON CRUSOE*

So grave, sententious, dogmatical a Rogue, that there is no enduring him.
Jonathan Swift

CHARLES DICKENS NOVELIST

If his novels are read at all in the future people will wonder what we saw in him.
George Meredith

Dickens seems to have succeeded in attacking everybody and antagonizing nobody.
George Orwell

I swallow Dickens whole and put up with the indigestion.
V.S. Pritchett

JAMES DICKEY NOVELIST, *DELIVERANCE*

The kind of man that after he has four martinis you want to drop a grenade down his throat.
Burt Reynolds

GORDON DICKSON WRITER

One of those singers with whom science fiction is cursed. Like Sprague De Camp and Poul Anderson, Gordie Dickson has a singing voice of which any walrus would be proud. **Isaac Asimov**

THEODORE DREISER NOVELIST

He was one of the most churlish, disagreeable men I ever met in my life, always thinking that everybody was cheating him.
Bennett Cerf

An Indiana peasant, snuffling absurdly over imbecile sentimentalities, giving a grave ear to quackeries, snorting and eye-rolling with the best of them...
H.L. Mencken

The reading of *Dawn* is a strain upon many parts, but the worst wear and tear fall upon the forearms.
Dorothy Parker

JOHN DRYDEN POET, PLAYWRIGHT

His imagination resembles the wings of an ostrich.

Thomas Babington Macaulay

His mind was of a slovenly character—fond of splendor, but indifferent to neatness. Hence most of his writings exhibit the sluttish magnificence of a Russian noble, all vermin diamonds, dirty linen and inestimable sables. **Thomas Babington Macaulay**

GEORGE ELIOT (MARY ANN EVANS) NOVELIST

I found out in the first two pages that it was a woman's writing— she supposed that in making a door you last of all put in the *panels*! **Thomas Carlyle**

George Eliot had the heart of Sappho; but the face, with the long proboscis, the protruding teeth of the Apocalyptic horse, betrayed animality. **George Meredith**

T.S. ELIOT POET, AUTHOR

...the cat-addict and cheese-taster, the writer of pawky blurbs, the church-warden, the polite deflater. **Cyril Connolly**

Every time I read a citation from him I am appalled by the triteness and banality of his utterances. **Henry Miller**

A company of actors inside one suit, each twitting the others.

V.S. Pritchett

Pale, marmoreal Eliot was there last week, like a chapped office boy on a high stool, with a cold in his head. **Virginia Woolf**

RALPH WALDO EMERSON POET, ESSAYIST

I could readily see in Emerson, not withstanding his merit, a gaping flaw. It was the insinuation that had he lived in those days when the world was made, he might have offered some valuable suggestions. **Herman Melville**

Emerson is one who lives instinctively on ambrosia—and leaves everything indigestible on his plate.　　**Friedrich Nietzsche**

WILLIAM FAULKNER NOVELIST, SHORT STORY WRITER

Even those who call Mr. Faulkner our greatest literary sadist do not fully appreciate him, for it is not merely his characters who have to run the gauntlet but also his readers.　　**Clifton Fadiman**

Mr. Faulkner, of course, is interested in making your mind rather than your flesh creep.　　**Clifton Fadiman**

Old Corndrinking Mellifluous.　　**Ernest Hemingway**

HENRY FIELDING NOVELIST, PLAYWRIGHT

Fielding had as much humor perhaps as Addison but, having no idea of grace, is perpetually disgusting.　　**Horace Walpole**

F. SCOTT FITZGERALD SHORT STORY WRITER, NOVELIST

I often feel about Fitzgerald that he couldn't distinguish between innocence and social climbing.　　**Saul Bellow**

He sees himself constantly not as a human being, but as a man in a novel or in a play. Every move is a picture and there is a camera man behind each tree.　　**Heywood Broun**

Mr. Fitzgerald…seems to believe that plagiarism begins at home.
　　Zelda Fitzgerald

The first of the last generation.　　**Gertrude Stein**

FORD MADOX FORD NOVELIST

His mind was like a Roquefort cheese, so ripe that it was palpably falling to pieces.　　**Van Wyck Brooks**

I had always avoided looking at Ford when I could and I always held my breath when I was near him in a closed room.
　　Ernest Hemingway

Hueffer was a flabby lemon and pink giant, who hung his mouth open as though he were an animal at the zoo inviting buns—especially when ladies were present. **Wyndham Lewis**

Master, mammoth mumbler. **Robert Lowell**

I once told Fordie that if he were placed naked and alone in a room without furniture I would come back in an hour and find total confusion. **Ezra Pound**

Freud Madox Fraud. **Osbert Sitwell**

E.M. FORSTER NOVELIST, SHORT STORY WRITER, ESSAYIST

E.M. Forster never gets any further than warming the teapot. He's a rare fine hand at that. Feel this teapot. Is it not beautifully warm? Yes, but there ain't going to be no tea. **Katherine Mansfield**

He's a mediocre man—and knows it, or suspects it, which is worse; he will come to no good, and in the meantime he's treated rudely by waiters and is not really admired even by middle-class dowagers. **Lytton Strachey**

ROBERT FROST POET

If it were thought that anything I wrote was influenced by Robert Frost I would take that particular piece of mine, shred it and flush it down the toilet, hoping not to clog the pipes. **James Dickey**

OLIVER GOLDSMITH POET, PLAYWRIGHT, NOVELIST

The misfortune of Goldsmith in conversation is this: he goes on without knowing how he is to get off. **Samuel Johnson**

THOMAS GRAY POET

Sir, he was dull in company, dull in his closet, dull everywhere. He was dull in a new way, and that made many people think him great. **Samuel Johnson**

ARTHUR HAILEY NOVELIST, *AIRPORT*

When book buyers buy books, they look for sex, violence and hard information. They get these from Arthur Hailey, whose characters discuss problems of hotel management while committing adultery before being beaten up. **Anthony Burgess**

DASHIELL HAMMETT MYSTERY NOVELIST

It was an unspoken pleasure, that having come together so many years, ruined so much and repaired a little, we had endured.

Lillian Hellman

Dashiell Hammett is as American as a sawed-off shotgun.... Brutal he is but his brutality, for what he must write, is clean and necessary, and there is in his work none of the smirking and swaggering savageries of a Hecht or a Bodenheim. **Dorothy Parker**

THOMAS HARDY NOVELIST, POET

Hardy went down to botanize in the swamps, while Meredith climbed toward the sun....Hardy became a sort of village atheist brooding and blaspheming over the village idiot.

G.K. Chesterton

The gloom is not even relieved by a little elegance of diction.

Lytton Strachey

FRANK HARRIS NOVELIST, JOURNALIST, AUTOBIOGRAPHER

Frank Harris is invited to all the great houses in London—once.

Oscar Wilde

JOEL CHANDLER HARRIS JOURNALIST, AUTHOR

In reality the stories are only alligator pears—one eats them merely for the sake of the dressing. **Mark Twain**

BRET HARTE JOURNALIST, AUTHOR

Harte, in a mild and colorless way, was that kind of man—that is
to say, he was a man without a country; no, not a man—man is
too strong a term; he was an invertebrate without a country.

Mark Twain

NATHANIEL HAWTHORNE NOVELIST, SHORT STORY WRITER

He never seemed to be doing anything and yet he did not like to
be disturbed at it. **John Greenleaf Whittier**

LILLIAN HELLMAN PLAYWRIGHT

Lillian Hellman is a homely woman, yet she moves as if she were
Marilyn Monroe. **Jane Fonda**

Every word she writes is a lie, including *and* and *the*.

Mary McCarthy

ERNEST HEMINGWAY NOVELIST, SHORT STORY WRITER

He is the bully on the Left Bank, always ready to twist the milk-
sop's arm. **Cyril Connolly**

He has never been known to use a word that might send the
reader to the dictionary. **William Faulkner**

I was the champ and when I read his stuff I knew he had something.
So I dropped a heavy glass skylight on his head at a drinking party.
But you can't kill the guy. He's not human. **F. Scott Fitzgerald**

Hemingway always rather disconcerted me—by eating the glass
after he'd had his drink. **Cary Grant**

When his cock wouldn't stand up he blew his head off. He sold
himself a line of bullshit and bought it. **Germaine Greer**

Hemingway's stupid book comes out and they make a big fuss out
of this old man and the stupid dead shark, and who cares?

Harold Robbins

Hemingway's remarks are not literature. **Gertrude Stein**

The secret of Ernest Hemingway's big sea catches is that he reels the fish to within twenty yards of his boat and then machine-guns them.   **Walter Winchell**

WILLIAM DEAN HOWELLS NOVELIST, POET, EDITOR

…the lousy cat of our letters.   **Ambrose Bierce**

VICTOR HUGO POET, NOVELIST, PLAYWRIGHT

A glittering humbug.   **Thomas Carlyle**

ALDOUS HUXLEY NOVELIST, ESSAYIST

People will call Mr. Aldous Huxley a pessimist; in the sense of one who makes the worst of it. To me he is that far more gloomy character; the man who makes the best of it.   **G.K. Chesterton**

Mr. Huxley is perhaps one of those people who have to perpetrate thirty bad novels before producing a good one.   **T.S. Eliot**

Do you notice that the more holy he gets, the more his books stink with sex. He cannot get off the subject of flagellating women.
                                                                        George Orwell

You could always tell by his conversation which volume of the *Encyclopedia Britannica* he'd been reading. One day it would be Alps, Andes and Apennines, and the next it would be the Himalayas and the Hippocratic Oath.   **Bertrand Russell**

All raw, uncooked, protesting.   **Virginia Woolf**

HENRIK IBSEN PLAYWRIGHT, POET

I began to hate Ibsen after *An Enemy of the People*; there's something insufferably aesthetic about him.   **August Strindberg**

HENRY JAMES NOVELIST, SHORT STORY WRITER

If Henry had cared more about a swimming pool and less about his dignity, he might not have spent his career at number 689 on the best-seller list.   **Russell Baker**

All I recall about Henry James is my mother complaining that he always wanted a lump of sugar broken in two for his tea—and that it really was affectation, as a small knob would do quite well.
Agatha Christie

A mind so fine that no idea could violate it.   **T.S. Eliot**

The nicest old lady I ever met.   **William Faulkner**

He confesses himself on every page....On every page James is a prude.   **George Moore**

When he isn't being a great and magnificent author he certainly can be a very fussy and tiresome one.   **Ezra Pound**

Mr. Henry James writes fiction as if it were a painful duty.
Oscar Wilde

SAMUEL JOHNSON CRITIC, POET

That pompous preacher of melancholy moralities.
Jeremy Bentham

There is no arguing with Johnson, for when his pistol misses fire he knocks you down with the butt.   **Oliver Goldsmith**

Johnson's aesthetic judgments are almost invariably subtle or solid or bold; they have always some good quality to recommend them—except one: they are never right.   **Lytton Strachey**

BEN JONSON POET, PLAYWRIGHT

Aristotle and the others haunted him...and stiffened a talent and a method already by nature sufficiently stiff.
Harley Granville-Barker

Reading him is like wading through glue.   **Alfred, Lord Tennyson**

JAMES JOYCE NOVELIST, SHORT STORY WRITER, POET

His writing is not about something. It is the thing itself.

Samuel Beckett

Ulysses is a dogged attempt to cover the universe with mud.

E.M. Forster

...so much of [*Ulysses*] consists of rather lengthy demonstrations of how a novel ought not to be written. **Aldous Huxley**

My God, what a clumsy *olla putrida* James Joyce is! Nothing but old fags and cabbage-stumps of quotations from the Bible and the rest, stewed in the juice of deliberate, journalistic dirty-mindedness. **D.H. Lawrence**

Probably Joyce thinks that because he prints all the dirty little words he is a great novelist. **George Moore**

...a man with a diseased mind and soul so black that he would even obscure the darkness of hell. **Reed Smoot**

He started off writing very well, then you can watch his going mad with vanity. He ends up a lunatic. **Evelyn Waugh**

...a queasy undergraduate scratching his pimples.

Virginia Woolf

IMMANUEL KANT PHILOSOPHER

Ever since Kant divorced reason from reality, his intellectual descendants have been diligently widening the breach. **Ayn Rand**

JOHN KEATS POET

That dirty little blackguard. **Lord Byron**

Such writing is mental masturbation...a Bedlam vision produced by raw pork and opium. **Lord Byron**

GARRISON KEILLOR HUMORIST, NOVELIST

I feel sorry for him because he has such a glorified opinion of himself.　　　　　　　　　　　　　　　　　**Bryant Gumbel**

KITTY KELLEY BIOGRAPHER

I hope the next time she is crossing a street four blind guys come along driving cars.　　　　　　　　　　　　　**Frank Sinatra**

JACK KEROUAC NOVELST, POET

That's not writing, that's typing.　　　　　　　**Truman Capote**

You know, I made it with Kerouac quite often.　　**Allen Ginsberg**

RUDYARD KIPLING NOVELST, POET, SHORT STORY WRITER

...stands for everything in this cankered world which I would wish were otherwise.　　　　　　　　　　　　**Dylan Thomas**

CHARLES LAMB ESSAYIST

Charles Lamb I sincerely believe to be in some considerable degree insane. A more pitiful, rickety, gasping, staggering, stammering Tomfool I do not know.　　　　　　　　　**Thomas Carlyle**

RING LARDNER HUMORIST, SHORT STORY WRITER

Jupiter on tiptoes.　　　　　　　　　　**Ernest Hemingway**

D.H. LAWRENCE NOVELIST, SHORT STORY WRITER, POET

His psychology of people is amazingly good up to a point, but at a certain point he gets misled by love of violent coloring.　　　　　　　　　　　　　　　　　**Bertrand Russell**

Mr. Lawrence looked like a plaster gnome on a stone toadstool in some suburban garden....He looked as if he had just returned from spending an uncomfortable night in a very dark cave, hiding, perhaps, in the darkness, from something which, at the same time, he on his side was hunting.   **Edith Sitwell**

TIMOTHY LEARY POLITICAL PROTESTER, AUTHOR

...creating a group of blissed-out pansies ripe for annihilation...
Abbie Hoffman

WYNDHAM LEWIS (PERCY WYNDHAM LEWIS)
NOVELIST, PAINTER

One of his minor purposes is to disembowel his enemies, who are numerous, for the simple reason that he wants them to be numerous.   **Arnold Bennett**

I do not think I have ever seen a nastier-looking man...Under the black hat, when I had first seen them, the eyes had been those of an unsuccessful rapist.   **Ernest Hemingway**

Mr. Lewis's pictures appeared...to have been painted by a mailed fist in a cotton glove.   **Edith Sitwell**

CLARE BOOTH LUCE JOURNALIST, PLAYWRIGHT

No woman of our time has gone further with less mental equipment.   **Clifton Fadiman**

THOMAS BABINGTON MACAULAY ESSAYIST, HISTORIAN

Macaulay is well for a while, but one wouldn't live under Niagara.   **Thomas Carlyle**

No person ever knew so much that was so little to the purpose.
Ralph Waldo Emerson

He not only overflowed with learning but stood in the slop.
Sydney Smith

NORMAN MAILER JOURNALIST, AUTHOR

. . .decocts matters of the first philosophical magnitude from an examination of his own ordure, and I am not talking about his books.   **William F. Buckley, Jr.**

KATHERINE MANSFIELD SHORT STORY WRITER

I loathe you. You revolt me stewing in your consumption. . . .You are a loathsome reptile—I hope you will die.   **D.H. Lawrence**

We could both wish that our first impression of K.M. was not that she stinks like a —well, civet cat that had taken to street-walking.
Virginia Woolf

SOMERSET MAUGHAM
NOVELIST, SHORT STORY WRITER, PLAYWRIGHT

Dialogue more tame than Wilde.   **Clive Barnes**

. . .a half-trashy novelist who writes badly but is patroized by half-serious readers who do not care much about wriing.
Edmund Wilson

CARSON McCULLERS NOVELIST, SHORT STORY WRITER

The somewhat puffy cheeks and vulnerable mouth and chin complete the expression of a sick wildcat caught in a parlor.
Cecil Beaton

Artistically gifted and humanly appalling.   **Gore Vidal**

HERMAN MELVILLE NOVELIST, SHORT STORY WRITER, POET

There is something slithery about him. . . .In his life they said he was mad—or crazy. But he was over the border. **D.H. Lawrence**

H.L. MENCKEN HUMORIST, AUTHOR, EDITOR

A small man so short in the thighs that when he stood up he seemed smaller than when he was sitting down.   **Alistair Cooke**

He edited a magazine called *The Smart Set*, which is like calling
Cape Kennedy "Lover's Lane."   **Ben Hecht**

With a pig's eyes that never look up, with a pig's snout that loves
muck, with a pig's brain that knows only the sty and a pig's
squeal that cries only when he is hurt, he sometimes opens
his pig's mouth, tusked and ugly, and lets out the voice of God,
railing at the whitewash that covers the manure about his habitat.
                                William Allen White

GEORGE MEREDITH NOVELIST, POET

What with the faking, what with the preaching, which was never
agreeable and is now said to be hollow, and what with the home
counties posing as the universe, it is no wonder Meredith now lies
in the trough.   **E.M. Forster**

Meredith is, to me, chiefly a stink. I should never write on him
as I detest him too much ever to trust myself as critic of him.
                                        Ezra Pound

GRACE METALIOUS NOVELIST

I want to make *The Grace Metalious Story*. She wrote *Peyton
Place*, became rich, bought Cadillacs and killed herself. That's a
great American story.   **John Waters**

JAMES MICHENER NOVELIST

Mr. Michener, as timeless as a stack of *National Geographics*, is
the ultimate Summer Writer. Just as one goes back to the cottage
in Maine, so one goes back to one's Michener.   **Wilfrid Sheed**

JOHN MILTON POET

Our language sunk under him.   **Joseph Addison**

The reason Milton wrote in fetters when he wrote of Angels
and God and at liberty when of the Devils and Hell, is because he
was a true poet, and of the Devil's party without knowing it.
                                        William Blake

...a silly coxcomb, fancifying himself a beauty; an unclean beast, with nothing more human about him than his guttering eyelids...

Claudius Salmasius

NANCY MITFORD NOVELIST

Nice cheap girl to take out for the evening. Costs you only eighteen-and-six for an orangeade in a night club. **Evelyn Waugh**

MOLIÈRE PLAYWRIGHT, ACTOR

Molière was a smart French plagiarist who hired three men to do his thinking for him. **D.W. Griffith**

GEORGE MOORE NOVELIST, PLAYWRIGHT, POET

George Moore unexpectedly pinched my behind. I felt rather honored that my behind should have drawn the attention of the great master of English prose. **Ilka Chase**

He leads his readers to the latrine and locks them in.

Oscar Wilde

MALCOLM MUGGERIDGE JOURNALIST, AUTHOR

Malcolm Muggeridge, a garden gnome expelled from Eden, has come to rest as a gargoyle brooding over a derelict cathedral.

Kenneth Tynan

VLADIMIR NABOKOV NOVELIST, POET

Mr. Nabokov is in the habit of introducing any job of this kind which he undertakes by the announcement that he is unique and incomparable and that everybody else who has attempted it is an oaf and ignoramus, usually with the implication that he is also a low-class person and a ridiculous personality. **Edmund Wilson**

FRIEDRICH NIETZSCHE PHILOSOPHER, POET

An agile but unintelligent and abnormal German, possessed of the mania of grandeur. **Leo Tolstoy**

CLIFFORD ODETS PLAYWRIGHT, FILM DIRECTOR

I don't think writers who cry about not having had a bicycle when they were kiddies are ever going to amount to much.

Dashiell Hammett

JOHN O'HARA NOVELIST, *BUTTERFIELD 8*

He lives in a perpetual state of just having discovered that it's a lousy world.

F. Scott Fitzgerald

CAMILLE PAGLIA CONTROVERSIAL "NEO-FEMINIST" AUTHOR

Get this woman a Valium! Hand her a gin!

Molly Ivins

DOROTHY PARKER SHORT STORY WRITER, POET, HUMORIST, CRITIC

The wit was never as attractive as the comment, often startling, always sudden, as if a curtain had opened and you had a brief and brilliant glance into what you would never have found for yourself.

Lillian Hellman

So odd a blend of Little Nell and Lady Macbeth.

Alexander Woollcott

ARTHUR WING PINERO PLAYWRIGHT, ACTOR, ESSAYIST

His eyebrows look like the skins of some small mammal just not large enough to be used as mats.

Max Beerbohm

SYLVIA PLATH POET

The Judy Garland of American poetry.

James Dickey

PLATO PHILOSOPHER

Take from him his sophisms, futilities and incomprehensibilities and what remains? His foggy mind.

Thomas Jefferson

Plato is a bore.

Friedrich Nietzsche

EDGAR ALLAN POE SHORT STORY WRITER, POET

...an unmanly sort of man whose love-life seems to have been largely confined to crying in laps and playing house. **W.H. Auden**

He was an adventurer into the vaults and cellars and horrible underground passages of the human soul. He sounded the horror and the warning of his own doom.   **D.H. Lawrence**

Three-fifths of him genius and two-fifths sheer fudge. **J.R. Lowell**

ALEXANDER POPE POET, SATIRIST

He hardly drank tea without a stratagem.   **Samuel Johnson**

Careless thinking carefully versified.   **J.R. Lowell**

If you looked at him he would spit poison and he would wind himself into an endless mesh-work of intrigues and suspicions if you did not.   **Lytton Strachey**

There are two ways of disliking poetry. One way is to dislike it, the other is to read Pope.   **Oscar Wilde**

EZRA POUND POET

Mr. Pound is humane, but not human.   **e.e. cummings**

To me Pound remains the exquisite showman minus the show.   **Ben Hecht**

A village explainer—excellent if you were a village, but if you were not, not.   **Gertrude Stein**

MARCEL PROUST NOVELIST

I think he was mentally defective.   **Evelyn Waugh**

Reading Proust is like bathing in someone else's dirty water.   **Alexander Woollcott**

HAROLD ROSS FOUNDER/EDITOR, *THE NEW YORKER*

Will you kindly inform the moron who runs your motion picture department that I did not write the movie entitled *Classified?* Neither did I write any of its wisecracking titles. Also inform him that Moses did not write the motion picture entitled *The Ten Commandments.*

Edna Ferber

DANTE GABRIEL ROSSETTI POET, PAINTER

The Rossetti Exhibition. I have been to see it and am pleased to find it more odious than I had even dared to hope.

Samuel Butler

A prince among parasites.

James McNeill Whistler

JEAN-JACQUES ROUSSEAU PHILOSOPHER, AUTHOR

I am heartily ashamed of anything I ever wrote in his favor.

David Hume

DAMON RUNYON SHORT STORY WRITER, JOURNALIST

Runyon was a mean-looking little guy. A statue of him would even scare off pigeons.

H. Allen Smith

BERTRAND RUSSELL MATHEMATICIAN, PHILOSOPHER, AUTHOR

One lady whose testimony is to be trusted made the shivering confession that the groping of the noble lord in an automobile conveyed the sensation of "dry leaves rustling up your thighs."

Alistair Cooke

VITA (VICTORIA) SACKVILLE-WEST NOVELIST, POET

She looks like Lady Chatterley above the waist and the game-keeper below.

Cyril Connolly

J.D. SALINGER NOVELIST, SHORT STORY WRITER

The greatest mind ever to stay in prep school.

Norman Mailer

GEORGE SAND (AURORE DUPIN) NOVELIST

A great cow full of ink.   **Gustave Flaubert**

CARL SANDBURG AUTHOR, POET

The poet lariat of Chicago.   **Richard J. Daley**

…a pacifist between wars.   **Robert Frost**

The cruelest thing that has happened to Lincoln since being shot by Booth was to have fallen into the hands of Carl Sandburg.
Edmund Wilson, reviewing Sandburg's biography of Lincoln

GEORGE SANTAYANA POET, PHILOSOPHER

He stood on the flat road to heaven and buttered slides to hell for all the rest.   **Oliver Wendell Holmes**

WILLIAM SAROYAN NOVELIST, SHORT STORY WRITER, PLAYWRIGHT

My father never liked me or my sister, and he never liked our mother, either, after an initial infatuation. In fact, he never liked anyone at all after an hour or two.   **Aram Saroyan**

DOROTHY L. SAYERS MYSTERY NOVELIST

Her slickness in writing has blinded many readers to the fact that her stories, considered as detective stories, are very bad ones…the crime is always committed in a way that is incredibly tortuous and quite uninteresting.   **George Orwell**

In any serious department of fiction, her writing would not appear to have any distinction at all.   **Edmund Wilson**

FRIEDRICH VON SCHILLER POET, PLAYWRIGHT, HISTORIAN

Schiller's blank verse is bad. He moves in it as a fly in a glue bottle.   **Samuel Taylor Coleridge**

WALTER SCOTT NOVELIST, POET, HISTORIAN

The public has done for good with the slipshod methods of amateur literary hacks like Scott.   **Ford Madox Ford**

Did he know how to write English and didn't do it because he didn't want to?   **Mark Twain**

…merely rhyming nonsense.   **William Wordsworth**

ERICH SEGAL NOVELIST

You had a choice of either being a knave or a fool, and you seem to have opted for both.   **John Simon**

WILLIAM SHAKESPEARE POET, PLAYWRIGHT

I have suffered more ghastly evenings with Shakespeare than with any other dramatist.   **Peter Brook**

I can hardly think it was the Stratford boy. Whoever wrote [the plays] had an aristocratic personality.   **Charlie Chaplin**

I have tried lately to read Shakespeare and found it so intolerably dull that it nauseated me.   **Charles Darwin**

We can say of Shakespeare that never has a man turned so little knowledge to such great account.   **T.S. Eliot**

If we wish to know the force of human genius we should read Shakespeare. If we wish to see the insignificance of human learning we may study his commentators.   **William Hazlitt**

Playing Shakespeare is very tiring. You never get to sit down unless you're a king.   **Josephine Hull**

Shakespeare never had six lines together without a fault. Perhaps you may find seven, but this does not refute my general assertion.
                                                    Samuel Johnson

When I read Shakespeare I am struck with wonder
That such trivial people should muse and thunder
In such lovely language.

                                                    D.H. Lawrence

His poetry has been cut into minute indigestible fragments and used like wedding cake, not to eat but to dream upon.

Walter Raleigh

It would positively be a relief to me to dig him up and throw stones at him. **George Bernard Shaw**

I think Shakespeare is shit! "Thee" and "thou"—the guy sounds like a faggot. **Gene Simmons**

I don't do Shakespeare. I don't talk in that kind of broken English. **Mr. T**

The undisputed fame enjoyed by Shakespeare as a writer...is, like every other lie, a great evil. **Leo Tolstoy**

Now we sit through Shakespeare in order to recognize the quotations. **Orson Welles**

GEORGE BERNARD SHAW PLAYWRIGHT, CRITIC

He uses the English language like a truncheon. **Max Beerbohm**

When you were quite a little boy somebody ought to have said "hush" just once. **Mrs. Patrick Campbell**

...the first man to have cut a swath through the theatre and left it strewn with virgins. **Frank Harris**

A freakish homunculus germinated outside lawful procreation.

Henry Arthur Jones

Too much gas-bag. **D.H. Lawrence**

It is his life work to announce the obvious in terms of the scandalous. **H.L. Mencken**

He writes his plays for the ages—the ages between five and twelve. **George Jean Nathan**

Shaw writes like a Pakistani who has learned English when he was twelve years old in order to become an accountant.

John Osborne

I remember coming across him at the Grand Canyon and finding him peevish, refusing to admire it or even look at it properly. He was jealous of it. **J.B. Priestley**

A blue-rumped ape. **Theodore Roosevelt**

Bernard Shaw had discovered himself and gave ungrudgingly of his discovery to the world. **Saki**

George Too Shaw To Be Good. **Dylan Thomas**

An idiot child screaming in a hospital. **H.G. Wells**

Bernard Shaw is an excellent man; he has not an enemy in the world, and none of his friends like him. **Oscar Wilde**

The way Bernard Shaw believes in himself is very refreshing in these atheistic days when so many people believe in no God at all. **Israel Zangwill**

PERCY BYSSHE SHELLEY POET

He had a fire in his eye, a fever in his blood, a maggot in his brain, a hectic flutter in his speech, which mark out the philosophic fanatic. **William Hazlitt**

A lewd vegetarian. **Charles Kingsley**

His voice was the most obnoxious squeak I ever was tormented with. **Charles Lamb**

Shelley should not be read but inhaled through a gas pipe.
Lionel Trilling

SAM SHEPARD PLAYWRIGHT, ACTOR

He is a very selfish, self-orientated person. **Robert Altman**

With *States of Shock* Sam Shepard appears to have finally attained what he was aiming at all along: total incomprehensibility. **John Simon**

EDITH SITWELL POET, NOVELIST

I am fairly unrepentant about her poetry. I really think that three-quarters of it is gibberish. However, I must crush down these thoughts, otherwise the dove of peace will shit on me.
Noël Coward

Then Edith Sitwell appeared, her nose longer than an anteater's, and read some of her absurd stuff.   **Lytton Strachey**

Isn't she a poisonous thing of a woman, lying, concealing, flipping, plagiarizing, misquoting and being as clever a crooked literary publicist as ever.   **Dylan Thomas**

...to whom I am as appreciatively indifferent as I am to the quaint patterns of old chintzes, the designs on dinner plates or the charm of nursery rhymes.   **H.G. Wells**

C.P. SNOW NOVELIST, SCIENTIST

He doesn't know what he means and doesn't know he doesn't know.
F.R. Leavis

SOCRATES PHILOSOPHER

The more I read about him, the less I wonder that they poisoned him.   **Thomas Babington Macaulay**

Socrates belonged to the lowest of the low: he was the mob. You can still see for yourself how ugly he was.   **Friedrich Nietzsche**

ALEXANDER SOLZHENITSYN NOVELIST

If Solzhenitsyn moved to L.A., within a few months he'd have a hot tub, be doing TM, be writing a movie and probably have two wives.   **Paul Mazursky**

The Russians displayed uncharacteristic humor in letting this nut come to our shores.   **Gore Vidal**

HERBERT SPENCER PHILOSOPHER

The most unending ass in Christendom.   **Thomas Carlyle**

STEVEN SPENDER POET

To see him fumbling with our rich and delicate language is to experience all the horror of seeing a Sèvres vase in the hands of a chimpanzee.

Evelyn Waugh

GERTRUDE STEIN AUTHOR

Miss Stein was a past master in making nothing happen very slowly.

Clifton Fadiman

Gertrude Stein is the mama of dada.

Clifton Fadiman

What an old covered-wagon she is!

F. Scott Fitzgerald

I was just thinking about Gertrude. She was ugly, fat, and a lesbian, but she collected more loot than all the jewels of Liz Taylor, Marlene and mine rolled together.

Paulette Goddard

She got to look like a Roman emperor, and that was fine if you liked your women to look like Roman emperors.

Ernest Hemingway

Gertrude Stein and me were just like brothers.

Ernest Hemingway

This has been a most wonderful evening. Gertrude has said things tonight it will take her ten years to understand.   **Alice B. Toklas**

In her last days Gertrude Stein resembled a spoiled pear.

Gore Vidal

JOHN STEINBECK NOVELIST, SHORT STORY WRITER

Hemingway tells me he doesn't think you're all that good a writer.

Humphrey Bogart

I can't read ten pages of Steinbeck without throwing up.

James Gould Cozzens

TOM STOPPARD PLAYWRIGHT, FILM DIRECTOR

What's *Rosencrantz and Guildenstern Are Dead* about? One woman on opening night came up to Tom Stoppard and said, "What is your play about?" And he said, "It is about to make me very rich."
Gary Oldman

HARRIET BEECHER STOWE NOVELIST

Uncle Tom's Cabin was the first evidence to America that no hurricane can be so disastrous to a country as a ruthlessly humanitarian woman.
Sinclair Lewis

A blatant Bassarid of Boston, a rampant Maenad of Massachusetts.
Algernon Swinburne

JACQUELINE SUSANN NOVELIST

A fright wig on a closed umbrella!
Mr. (Earl) Blackwell

She looks like a truck driver in drag.
Truman Capote

For the reader who has put away comic books but isn't ready yet for editorials in the *Daily News*.
Gloria Steinem

JONATHAN SWIFT POET, POLITICAL SATIRIST

A monster gibbering shrieks, and gnashing imprecations against mankind—tearing down all shreds of modesty, past all sense of manliness and shame; filthy in word, filthy in thought, furious, raging, obscene.
William Makepeace Thackeray

ALGERNON SWINBURNE POET

As to Swinburne's verses...they are "florid impotence", to my taste, the *minimum* of thought and idea in the *maximum* of words and phraseology.
Robert Browning

...sitting in a sewer and adding to it.
Thomas Carlyle

IDA TARBELL JOURNALIST, BIOGRAPHER

Miss Tarbarrel.

John D. Rockefeller

ALFRED, LORD TENNYSON POET

There was little about melancholia that he didn't know; there was little else that he did.

W.H. Auden

To think of him dribbling his powerful intellect through the gimlet holes of poetry!

Thomas Carlyle

Tennyson is a beautiful half of a poet.

Ralph Waldo Emerson

I would he were as his poems.

Edward Lear

WILLIAM MAKEPEACE THACKERAY NOVELIST

Thackeray settled like a meat-fly on whatever one had got for dinner and made one sick of it.

John Ruskin

DYLAN THOMAS POET

Thomas was an outstandingly unpleasant man, one who cheated and stole from his friends and peed on their carpets.

Kingsley Amis

In America, visiting British writers are greeted at cocktail parties by faculty wives with "Can you screw as good as Dylan?"

Anthony Burgess

I asked Dylan Thomas why he'd come to Hollywood and very solemnly he said, "To touch a starlet's tits." "OK," I said, "but only one finger."

Shelley Winters

HENRY DAVID THOREAU POET, ESSAYIST

He liked to administer doses of moral quinine, and he never thought of sugaring his pills.

Van Wyck Brooks

He was imperfect, unfinished, inartistic; he was worse than provincial—he was parochial.

Henry James

JAMES THURBER ESSAYIST, SHORT STORY WRITER, HUMORIST

Some drunk dame told Jim at a party that she would like to have a baby by him. Jim said, "Surely you don't mean by unartificial insemination!" **Nunnally Johnson**

Thurber did not write the way a surgeon operates, he wrote the way a child skips rope, the way a mouse waltzes. **E.B. White**

LEO TOLSTOY NOVELIST

I took a speed-reading course and read *War and Peace* in twenty minutes. It involves Russia. **Woody Allen**

MARK TWAIN HUMORIST, NOVELIST, JOURNALIST

He had one of the more wicked minds ever going. **Truman Capote**

...tricked out a few of the old proven "sure fire" literary skeletons with sufficient local color to intrigue the superficial and the lazy. **William Faulkner**

Mark Twain and I are in very much the same position. We have to put things in such a way as to make people, who would otherwise hang us, believe that we are joking. **George Bernard Shaw**

GORE VIDAL NOVELIST, PLAYWRIGHT, ESSAYIST, SHORT STORY WRITER

He's a much better conversationalist than he is a writer. *Myra Breckenridge* wasn't even good pornography. **Ian Shoales**

ALICE WALKER NOVELIST, POET, SHORT STORY WRITER

I told her I would play a Venetian blind, dirt on the floor, anything. **Whoopi Goldberg**

EVELYN WAUGH NOVELIST

Evelyn's abiding complex and the source of much of his misery was that he was not a six-foot-tall, extremely handsome and rich duke. **Cecil Beaton**

He looked, I decided, like a letter delivered to the wrong address.
Malcolm Muggeridge

A disgusting common little man…he had never been taught how to avoid being offensive.
Rebecca West

His style has the desperate jauntiness of an orchestra fiddling away for dear life on a sinking ship.
Edmund Wilson

H.G. WELLS SCI-FI NOVELIST, JOURNALIST

Whatever he writes is not only alive, but kicking.
Henry James

I stopped thinking about him when he became a thinker.
Lytton Strachey

The Old Maid among novelists.
Rebecca West

REBECCA WEST JOURNALIST, CRITIC, NOVELIST

She writes like a loom, producing her broad rich fabric with hardly a thought of how it will make up into a shape, while I write to cover a frame of ideas.
H.G. Wells

WALT WHITMAN POET

This poet with the private soul leaking out of him all the time. All his privacy leaking out in a sort of dribble, oozing into the universe.
D.H. Lawrence

…interesting even where he is grotesque or perverse.
George Santayana

He is a writer of something occasionally like English, and a man of something occasionally like genius.
Algernon Swinburne

OSCAR WILDE POET, PLAYWRIGHT, NOVELIST

That sovereign of insufferables.
Ambrose Bierce

What a tiresome, affected sod.
Noël Coward

He festooned the dung heap on which he had placed himself with sonnets as people grow honeysuckle around outdoor privies.
Quentin Crisp

Oscar Wilde's talent seems to me essentially rootless, something growing in a glass in a little water.
George Moore

> When Oscar came to join his God,
> Not earth to earth but sod to sod,
> It was for sinners such as this,
> Hell was created bottomless.
>
> **Algernon Swinburne**

Oscar Wilde was overdressed, pompous, snobbish, sentimental and vain.
Evelyn Waugh

TENNESSEE WILLIAMS PLAYWRIGHT

If a swamp alligator could talk, it would sound like Tennessee Williams.
Rex Reed

P.G. WODEHOUSE AUTHOR, HUMORIST

English Literature's performing flea.
Sean O'Casey

TOM WOLFE NOVELIST, *BONFIRE OF THE VANITIES*

In my mind there is something silly about a man who wears a white suit all the time, especially in New York.
Norman Mailer

MARY WOLLSTONECRAFT FEMINIST WRITER

…that hyena in petticoats.
Horace Walpole

VIRGINIA WOOLF NOVELIST

Virginia Woolf's writing is no more than glamorous knitting. I believe she must have a pattern somewhere.
Edith Sitwell

She had been a peculiar kind of snob without really belonging to a social group with whom to be snobbish.
Edmund Wilson

ALEXANDER WOOLLCOTT JOURNALIST, CRITIC, AUTHOR

...the New Jersey Nero who mistakes his pinafore for a toga.

Edna Ferber

...a persnickety fellow with more fizz than brain.   **Ben Hecht**

He seemed to feel a need to find the minutest chinks in his friends' armor, wherein to insert a poisoned needle.   **John Keats**

He looked like something that had gotten loose from Macy's Thanksgiving Day Parade.   **Harpo Marx**

You, sir, are the lowest form of life—a cribbage pimp.

Alice Duer Miller

...a fat duchess with the emotions of a fish.   **Harold Ross**

Old Vitriol and Violets.   **James Thurber**

...a butterfly in heat.   **Louis Untermeyer**

WILLIAM WORDSWORTH POET

The great Metaquizzical poet.   **Lord Byron**

For prolixity, thinness, endless dilution, it excels all the other speech I had heard from mortals....The languid way in which he gives you a handful of numb unresponsive fingers is very significant.   **Thomas Carlyle**

Is Wordsworth a bell with a wooden tongue?

Ralph Waldo Emerson

Mr. Wordsworth, a very stupid man with a decided gift for portraying nature in vignette, never yet ruined anyone's morals unless, perhaps, he has driven some susceptible persons to crime in a very fury of boredom.   **Ezra Pound**

ÉMILE ZOLA AUTHOR, CRITIC

His work is evil, and he is one of those unhappy beings of whom one can say that it would be better had he never been born.

Anatole France

Mr. Zola is determined to show that if he has not genius he can at least be dull.

Oscar Wilde

CHAPTER FIVE

POLITICALLY INCORRECT

"Suppose you were an idiot,
and suppose you were a member of Congress,
but I repeat myself."

MARK TWAIN

BELLA ABZUG U.S. CONGRESSWOMAN

Republicans should work for adoption of environmental programs, welfare and revenue-sharing, and most importantly we have to keep Bella Abzug from showing up in Congress in hotpants.
Spiro Agnew

SPIRO AGNEW FORMER U.S. VICE-PRESIDENT

I hesitate to get into the gutter with this guy.
Chet Huntley

Mr. Agnew tells us that we lack a sense of humor. I think he is doing his best to restore it.
Edmund Muskie

Thank God nobody ever accused me of raising Spiro Agnew.
Dr. Benjamin Spock

PRINCESS ANNE (1950–) BRITISH ROYAL

Such an active lass. So outdoorsy. She loves nature in spite of what it did to her.
Bette Midler

QUEEN ANNE (1665–1714) BRITISH RULER

...when in good humor was meekly stupid and when in bad humor was sulkily stupid.
Thomas Babington Macaulay

BENEDICT ARNOLD U.S. ARMY OFFICER, TRAITOR

He seems to have been so hackneyed in villainy and so lost to all sense of honor and shame that while his facilities will enable him to continue his sordid pursuits, there will be no time for remorse.
George Washington

NANCY ASTOR FIRST FEMALE MEMBER OF BRITISH PARLIAMENT

Viscount Waldorf Astor owned Britain's two most influential newspapers, the *Times* and the *Observer*, but his American wife Nancy had a wider circulation than both papers put together.
Emery Kelen

CLEMENT ATTLEE ENGLISH PRIME MINISTER (1945–1951)

He is a sheep in sheep's clothing.   **Winston Churchill**

He reminds me of nothing so much as a dead fish before it has had time to stiffen.   **George Orwell**

THOMAS HART BENTON U.S. SENATOR, STATESMAN

…the doughty knight of the stuffed cravat.   **John Quincy Adams**

NAPOLEON BONAPARTE FRENCH SOLDIER, EMPEROR

Bonaparte was a lion in the field only. In civil life a cold-blooded, calculating, unprincipled usurper without a virtue; no states-man, knowing nothing of commerce, political economy or civil government, and supplying ignorance by bold presumption.
          Thomas Jefferson

He is no gentleman.   **Arthur Wellesley, Duke of Wellington**

BILL BRADLEY BASKETBALL PLAYER, U.S. SENATOR

Bradley has all the charisma of gravel.   **Dave Barry**

JERRY BROWN U.S. POLITICIAN, GOVERNOR OF CALIFORNIA

Lord of the flies.   **Gore Vidal**

WILLIAM JENNINGS BRYAN U.S. POLITICIAN, SECRETARY OF STATE

With him, words take the place of actions.   **Henry Cabot Lodge**

The national tear duct.   **H.L. Mencken**

He can take a batch of words and scramble them together and leaven them properly with a hunk of oratory and knock the White House doorknob right out of a candidate's hand.
          Will Rogers

He is *absolutely* sincere. That is what makes him dangerous.
          Theodore Roosevelt

WILLIAM F. BUCKLEY, JR.
MAGAZINE (*NATIONAL REVIEW*) FOUNDER/EDITOR, POLITICAL COMMENTATOR

It's great to be with Bill Buckley, because you don't have to think. He takes a position and you automatically take the opposite one and you know you're right.   **John Kenneth Galbraith**

He does not speak as much as exhale, and he exhales polysyllabically.   **Edwin Newman**

He uses too big a words.   **Ronald Reagan**

Probably the only person in the world who would work in a word like *solipsistic*—while calling his dog.   **Mark Russell**

I think Buckley's a fool who spends too much time caressing dictionaries.   **Ian Shoales**

Looks and sounds not unlike Hitler, but without the charm.
Gore Vidal

BARBARA BUSH   U.S. FIRST LADY

What's wrong with looking sixty instead of looking like an anorexic twelve-year-old?   **Faith Popcorn**

Barbara Bush reads *House and Garden* for fashion tips.
Judy Tenuta

GEORGE BUSH   41ST U.S. PRESIDENT

My family got all over me because they said Bush is only for the rich people. Then I reminded them, "Hey, I'm rich."
Charles Barkley

A pin-stripin', polo-playin', umbrella-totin' Ivy-Leaguer, born with a silver spoon so far back in his mouth that you couldn't get it out with a crowbar.   **Bill Baxley**

George Bush says he hears the quiet people others don't. I have a friend in Los Angeles who hears the quiet people others don't and he has to take a lot of medication for it.   **Albert Brooks**

You know, Bush is always comparing me to Elvis [Presley] in sort of unflattering ways. I don't think Bush would have liked Elvis very much, and that's just another thing that's wrong with him.
Bill Clinton

All hat and no cattle.
John Connally

Well excuse me, George Herbert irregular-heart-beating, read-my-lying-lipping, sipping-in-the-pool, do-nothing, deficit-raising, make-less-money-than-Millie-the-White-House-dog-last-year, Quayle-loving, sushi-puking Walker Bush.
Arsenio Hall

If ignorance ever goes to forty dollars a barrel, I want drilling rights on George Bush's head.
Jim Hightower

George Bush is anti-abortion and pro-capital punishment. With him it's just a matter of timing.
Dennis Miller

George Bush is Gerald Ford without the pizzazz.
Pat Paulsen

He doesn't seem to stand for anything.
Ronald Reagan

He can't help himself. He was born with a silver foot in his mouth.
Ann Richards

He has the look about him of someone who might sit up and yip for a Dog Yummie.
Mike Royko

I think George Bush belongs to Jehovah's Bystanders. When his plane went down in World War II his whole life flashed before him, and he wasn't in it.
Mort Sahl

BILLY CARTER
PEANUT FARMER, BROTHER OF U.S. PRESIDENT JIMMY CARTER

Jimmy needs Billy like Van Gogh needs stereo.
Johnny Carson

Billy's doing his share for the economy. He's put the beer industry back on its feet.
Jimmy Carter

Whenever there's trouble, that's where Billy is. Sometimes when I look at all my children I say to myself, "Lillian, you should have stayed a virgin."
Lillian Carter

JIMMY CARTER 39TH U.S. PRESIDENT

Everybody seems to be disappointed in Jimmy Carter. The other day Miz Lillian was heard muttering, "To think I voted for him."
Joey Adams

Jimmy Carter came from a simple, God-fearing homespun southern family that was normal in every respect except that many of its members, upon close inspection, appeared to be crazy. After graduating from the U.S. Naval Academy he served as an officer aboard a nuclear submarine where, due to an unfortunate radiation leakage, he developed enormous mutant teeth. **Dave Barry**

Jimmy used to drink liquor. Now he's running for president and he drinks Scotch, and I've never trusted a Scotch drinker.
Billy Carter

A chicken-fried McGovern. **Robert Dole**

I take that back because I've come to respect McGovern.
Robert Dole

I think Jimmy Carter as president is like Truman Capote marrying Dolly Parton. The job is just too big for him. **Rich Little**

If you're in the peanut business, you learn to think small.
Eugene McCarthy

Depression is when you are out of work. A recession is when your neighbor is out of work. A recovery is when Jimmy Carter is out of work. **Ronald Reagan**

Carter is the best president the Soviet Union ever had.
William Safire

FIDEL CASTRO CUBAN DICTATOR

All I know about Cuba is they've got some scruffy-looking guy running the country who smokes a cigar. **Charles Barkley**

NEVILLE CHAMBERLAIN ENGLISH PRIME MINISTER

He has the lucidity which is the by-product of a fundamentally
sterile mind. **Aneurin Bevan**

Neville Chamberlain looked at foreign affairs through the wrong
end of a municipal drainpipe. **Winston Churchill**

WINSTON CHURCHILL BRITISH STATESMAN, AUTHOR

Churchill had the habit of breaking the rungs of any ladder he
put his foot on. **Lord Beaverbrook**

He would rather make love to a word than a woman.
Ingrid Bergman

I welcome this opportunity of pricking the bloated bladder of lies
with the poniard of truth. **Aneurin Bevan**

When I am right, I get angry. Churchill gets angry when he is
wrong. We are angry at each other much of the time.
Charles De Gaulle

He would make a drum out of the skin of his own mother in order
to sound his own praises. **David Lloyd George**

He has spoilt himself by reading about Napoleon.
David Lloyd George

It is fun being in the same decade with you. **Franklin Roosevelt**

GROVER CLEVELAND 22ND AND 24TH U.S. PRESIDENT

His whole huge carcass seemed to be made of iron....He sailed
through American history like a steel ship loaded with monoliths
of granite. **H.L. Mencken**

His Accidency. **Theodore Roosevelt**

BILL CLINTON 42ND U.S. PRESIDENT

This is the first president who's not old enough to be my father. Who understood rock 'n' roll, who smoked dope, definitely fucked that blonde and avoided the draft. He did the things that I can relate to. **Jon Bon Jovi**

The Prince of Sleaze. **Jerry Brown**

Bill Clinton's foreign policy experience stems mainly from having breakfast at the International House of Pancakes. **Pat Buchanan**

First one side [of an issue], then the other. He's been spotted in more places than Elvis Presley. **George Bush**

Oh, I long for my monologue when Clinton has a bad hair day. **Johnny Carson**

Bill looks a lot better when he's not wearing those running shorts. **Cindy Crawford**

If any more Clinton relatives come out of the woodwork, they're gonna have to change the presidential theme from "Hail to the Chief" to "We Are Family." **Jay Leno**

Did you see the pictures in the newspapers of President Clinton on the beach in Hawaii? I thought it was an ad for *Free Willy*! **Dennis Miller**

CALVIN COOLIDGE 30TH U.S. PRESIDENT

The greatest man who ever came out of Plymouth Corner, Vermont. **Clarence Darrow**

He looks as if he had been weaned on a pickle. **Alice Roosevelt Longworth**

...a dreadful little cad. **H.L. Mencken**

Calvin Coolidge didn't say much, and when he did he didn't say much. **Will Rogers**

MARIO CUOMO GOVERNOR OF NEW YORK

Yecch. **Ed Koch**

Liberalism's sensitive philosopher king. **Dan Quayle**

JEFFERSON DAVIS CONFEDERATE PRESIDENT

Ambitious as Lucifer and cold as a lizard. **Sam Houston**

CHARLES DE GAULLE FRENCH SOLDIER, STATESMAN

He is like a female llama surprised in her bath.

Winston Churchill

An artlessly sincere megalomaniac. **H.G. Wells**

DENG XIAOPING CHINESE POLITICAL LEADER

…[an] 85-year-old chain-smoking Communist dwarf.

Pat Buchanan

EAMON DE VALERA IRISH PRIME MINISTER, PRESIDENT

He is like trying to pick up mercury with a fork.

David Lloyd George

DIANA PRINCESS OF WALES

Princess Di wears more clothes in one day than Gandhi wore in his whole life. **Joan Rivers**

DAVID DINKINS NEW YORK CITY MAYOR

A fancy schvartze with a moustache. **Jackie Mason**

ROBERT DOLE U.S. SENATOR

It's Dole's misfortune that when he does smile, he looks as if he's just evicted a widow. **Mike Royko**

STEPHEN A. DOUGLAS U.S. SENATOR

Douglas can never be president, Sir....His legs are too short, Sir. His coat, like a cow's tail, hangs too near the ground, Sir.
Thomas Hart Benton

His argument is as thin as the homeopathic soup that was made by boiling the shadow of a pigeon that had been starved to death.
Abraham Lincoln

MICHAEL DUKAKIS
PRESIDENTIAL CANDIDATE, GOVERNOR OF MASSACHUSETTS

He's the only man I know who could look at the swimsuit issue of *Sports Illustrated* and complain because the bathing suits weren't flame-retardant.
James Baker

He's the Stealth candidate....His campaign jets from place to place but no issues show up on the radar screen.
George Bush

...Michael Dukakis, oh boy. Popularity really plummeting there. In fact, even Willie Horton is claiming, "Look, I hardly even knew the guy."
Jay Leno

Want to hear a sad story about the Dukakis campaign? The governor of Massachusetts, he lost his top naval adviser last week. The rubber duck drowned in his bathtub.
Dan Quayle

JOHN FOSTER DULLES U.S. SECRETARY OF STATE

...the only bull I ever knew who carried his own china shop around with him.
Winston Churchill

ANTHONY EDEN ENGLISH PRIME MINISTER

He is not only a bore, but he bores for England.
Malcolm Muggeridge

EDWARD VIII KING OF ENGLAND (1936)

"You know," he once said to me with a smile, "I've got a low IQ."
Lilli Palmer

DWIGHT D. EISENHOWER 34TH U.S. PRESIDENT

I doubt very much if a man whose main literary interests were in works by Mr. Zane Grey, admirable as they may be, is particularly well-equipped to be chief executive of this country, particularly where Indian affairs are concerned.   **Dean Acheson**

The best clerk I ever fired.   **Douglas MacArthur**

Good man, wrong job.   **Sam Rayburn**

Not long ago it was proved that Dwight D. Eisenhower was descended from the royal line of Britain, a proof if one were needed that everyone is descended from everyone.   **John Steinbeck**

ELIZABETH I BRITISH QUEEN

As just and merciful as Nero and as good a Christian as Mahomet.   **John Wesley**

ELIZABETH II BRITISH QUEEN

She was like a Mum to us.   **John Lennon**

Queen Elizabeth is the whitest person in the world.   **Bette Midler**

In the early a.m. I was at the foot of her bed eating Rice Krispies.   **Dudley Moore**

Frumpish and banal.   **Malcolm Muggeridge**

FAROUK I KING OF EGYPT

At times he compelled my mother to smoke a big cigar. My mother didn't like tobacco and he knew it; he seemed to enjoy making her cough.   **Omar Sharif**

SARAH FERGUSON DUCHESS OF WINDSOR

She is a lady short on looks, absolutely deprived of any dress sense, has a figure like a Jurassic monster, is very greedy, [has] no tact and wants to upstage everyone else.   **Nicholas Fairbairn**

GERALD FORD 38TH U.S. PRESIDENT

Richard Nixon impeached himself. He gave us Gerald Ford as his revenge. **Bella Abzug**

The nuclear button was at one stage at the disposal of a man, Gerald Ford, who might have either pressed it by mistake or else pressed it deliberately to obtain room service. **Clive James**

Jerry Ford is so dumb that he can't fart and chew gum at the same time. **Lyndon Johnson**

If Ford can get away with this list of issues...and be elected on it, then I'm going to call the dictator of Uganda, Mr. Amin, and tell him to start giving speeches on airport safety. **Walter Mondale**

MAHATMA GANDHI PHILOSOPHER, INDIAN POLITICAL LEADER

It is alarming and also nauseating to see Mr. Gandhi, a seditious Middle Temple lawyer, now posing as a fakir of a type well known in the East, striding half-naked up the steps of the viceregal palace...to parley on equal terms with the representatives of the king-emperor. **Winston Churchill**

Gandhi has been assassinated. In my humble opinion a bloody good thing but far too late. **Noël Coward**

GEORGE III BRITISH KING (1760–1820)

An old, mad, blind, despised and dying king.
Percy Bysshe Shelley

WILLIAM GLADSTONE BRITISH PRIME MINISTER

Gladstone read Homer for fun, which I thought served him right.
Winston Churchill

He has not a single redeeming defect. **Benjamin Disraeli**

JOHN GLENN U.S. SENATOR, ASTRONAUT

He couldn't electrify a fish tank if he threw a toaster in it.
Dave Barry

POLITICALLY INCORRECT | 161

I told John it wasn't fair for him to take advantage of his hero status as an astronaut. I mentioned this at the unveiling of the portrait showing me invading Italy.   **Robert Dole**

BARRY GOLDWATER U.S. SENATOR, PRESIDENTIAL CANDIDATE

You're one of the handsomest men in America. You ought to be in the movies. In fact, I've made just that proposal to Eighteenth Century-Fox.   **Hubert Humphrey**

Barry Goldwater is standing on his record—that's so no one can see it.   **John F. Kennedy**

MIKHAIL GORBACHEV RUSSIAN POLITICAL LEADER

Comrades, this man has a nice smile, but he's got iron teeth.
                                              Andrey Gromyko

AL GORE U.S. VICE-PRESIDENT

He's got a wooden chin.   **Hillary Clinton**

ULYSSES S. GRANT U.S. MILITARY LEADER, 18TH U.S. PRESIDENT

He combined great gifts with great mediocrity. **Woodrow Wilson**

ALEXANDER HAMILTON U.S. STATESMAN

Now, he was the first Secretary of the Treasury. The reason he was appointed that was because he and Washington were the only men in America at that time who knew how to put their names on a check.   **Will Rogers**

WARREN G. HARDING 29TH U.S. PRESIDENT

A tin-horn politician with the manner of a rural corn doctor and the mien of a ham actor.   **H.L. Mencken**

If there ever was a he-harlot, it was this same Warren G. Harding.
                                          William Allen White

BENJAMIN HARRISON 23RD U.S. PRESIDENT

A cold-blooded, narrow-minded, obstinate, timid old psalm-singing politician. **Theodore Roosevelt**

GARY HART U.S. SENATOR

Gary Hart is just Jerry Brown without the fruit flies.

Robert Strauss

HENRY VIII BRITISH KING

The plain truth is that he was a most intolerable ruffian, a disgrace to human nature and a blot of blood and grease upon the History of England. **Charles Dickens**

ADOLF HITLER GERMAN DICTATOR

Maybe if I hadn't been so fastidious, I might have changed history. But, oh, that body odor of his. **Lina Basquette**

When you think about it, Adolf Hitler was the first pop star. It certainly wasn't his politics. He was a media pop star.

David Bowie

If Hitler invaded hell, I would make at least a favorable reference to the devil in the House of Commons. **Winston Churchill**

Hitler had the best answers to everything. **Charles Manson**

A psychopath who somehow found his way from a padded cell to Potsdam. **Malcolm Muggeridge**

The world is too small to provide adequate living for both Hitler and God. **Franklin Roosevelt**

A combination of initiative, perfidy and epilepsy. **Leon Trotsky**

ABBIE HOFFMAN U.S. POLITICAL ACTIVIST

Abbie had a charisma that must have come out of an immaculate conception between Fidel Castro and Groucho Marx. They went into his soul and he came out looking like an ethnic milkshake—Jewish revolutionary, Puerto Rican lord, Italian street kid, Black Panther with the old Afro haircut, even a glint of Irish gunman in the mad, green eyes.   **Norman Mailer**

HERBERT HOOVER 31ST U.S. PRESIDENT

In 1932, lame duck President Herbert Hoover was so desperate to remain in the White House that he dressed up as Eleanor Roosevelt. When FDR discovered the hoax in 1936, the two men decided to stay together for the sake of the children.
Johnny Carson

J. EDGAR HOOVER FBI HEAD

...whom you should trust as much as you would a rattlesnake with a silencer on its rattle.   **Dean Acheson**

...[a] killer fruit.   **Truman Capote**

It's probably better to have him inside the tent pissing out than outside the tent pissing in.   **Lyndon Johnson**

HUBERT HUMPHREY U.S. VICE-PRESIDENT

Hubert Humphrey talks so fast that listening to him is like trying to read *Playboy* magazine with your wife turning the pages.
Barry Goldwater

...a treacherous, brain-damaged old vulture....They don't hardly make 'em like Hubert anymore—but just to be on the safe side he should be castrated anyway.   **Hunter S. Thompson**

SADDAM HUSSEIN IRAQI DICTATOR

If we get into an armed situation he's going to get his ass kicked.
George Bush

If you think Saddam Hussein is a madman, you should meet his brothers Certifiably and Criminally.   **Johnny Carson**

If I could find a way to get him out of there, even putting a contract out on him, if the CIA did that sort of thing, assuming it ever did, I would be for it.   **Richard Nixon**

You know, when he was born they didn't give his mother a medical bill. They fined her for dumping toxic waste. **Ronald Reagan**

As far as Saddam Hussein being a great military strategist, he is neither a strategist nor is he schooled in operational arts. He's not a tactician. He's not a general. He's not a soldier. Other than that, he's a great military man.   **Norman Schwarzkopf**

ANDREW JACKSON 7TH U.S. PRESIDENT

A barbarian who could not write a sentence of grammar and hardly could spell his own name.   **John Quincy Adams**

JESSE JACKSON U.S. POLITICIAN, CIVIL RIGHTS ACTIVIST

A lot of people are questioning if Jesse is truly out there to lead in the highest moral sense or if he's out there for personal power and personal gain.   **Harry Belafonte**

The hustler from Chicago.   **George Bush**

Jesse Jackson is a man of the cloth. Cashmere.   **Mort Sahl**

THOMAS JEFFERSON 3RD U.S. PRESIDENT

His attachment to those of his friends whom he could make useful to himself was thoroughgoing and exemplary.

John Quincy Adams

ANDREW JOHNSON 17TH U.S. PRESIDENT

Johnson is an insolent drunken brute in comparison with which Caligula's horse was respectable.   **Charles Sumner**

LYNDON BAINES JOHNSON 36TH U.S. PRESIDENT

When Johnson wanted to persuade you of something you really felt as if a St. Bernard had licked your face for an hour.
Benjamin C. Bradlee

He is a man of his most recent word.   **William F. Buckley, Jr.**

Hyperbole was to Lyndon Johnson what oxygen is to life.
Bill Moyers

JOHN F. KENNEDY 35TH U.S. PRESIDENT

I have a curious and apprehensive feeling as I watch JFK that he is sort of an Indian snake charmer.   **Dean Acheson**

Everyone's talking about how young the candidates are. And it's true. A few months ago Kennedy's mother said, "You have a choice...do you want to go to camp this year or run for president?"
Bob Hope

Underneath the beautiful exterior there was an element of ruthlessness and toughness that I had trouble either accepting or forgetting.   **Hubert Humphrey**

Jack was out kissing babies while I was out passing bills. Someone had to tend the store.   **Lyndon Johnson**

I too slept with Jack Kennedy.   **Bette Midler**

Now he is a legend when he would have preferred to be a man.
Jacqueline Kennedy Onassis

It is said the President is willing to laugh at himself...when is he going to extend that privilege to us?   **Mort Sahl**

ROBERT F. KENNEDY U.S. SECRETARY OF STATE, ATTORNEY GENERAL

Robert Kennedy has a vigorous image—he has ten children. Everybody thinks that's because he's a devout Catholic. Not so— he's a sex maniac.   **Joey Adams**

...the highest-ranking withdrawn adolescent since Alexander Hamilton in 1794.   **Murray Kempton**

I just don't like that boy and I never will. He worked for old Joe McCarthy, you know, and when old Joe was tearing up the Constitution and the country, that boy couldn't say enough for him.   **Harry S Truman**

EDWARD M. (TEDDY) KENNEDY U.S. SENATOR

I admire Ted Kennedy. How many fifty-nine-year-olds do you know who still go to Florida for spring break?   **Pat Buchanan**

Senator McGovern was making a speech. He said, "Gentlemen, let me tax your memories." And Ted Kennedy jumped up and said, "Why haven't we thought of that before!"   **Robert Dole**

Every country should have at least one King Farouk. **Gore Vidal**

He would have made a very good bartender.   **Gore Vidal**

THE AYATOLLAH KHOMEINI IRANIAN RELIGIOUS LEADER

He leads the people into a daily deification of terrorism.
                                                Shah Reza Pahlavi

NIKITA KHRUSHCHEV RUSSIAN PREMIER (1958–1964)

Khrushchev reminds me of the tiger hunter who has picked a place on the wall to hang the tiger's skin long before he has caught the tiger. This tiger has other ideas.   **John F. Kennedy**

MARTIN LUTHER KING, JR. CIVIL RIGHTS ADVOCATE

He got the peace prize, we got the problem. I don't want the white man giving me medals.   **Malcolm X**

HENRY KISSINGER U.S. SECRETARY OF STATE

[He] became the nation's top foreign-policy strategist despite being born with the handicaps of a laughable accent and no morals or neck.   **Dave Barry**

Henry's idea of sex is to slow the car down to thirty miles an hour when he drops you off at the door.

Barbara Howar

Peter Sellers' most deadly deft mimic.

Studs Terkel

The smell of his dirty socks was overpowered by his denture breath.

Mamie Van Doren

ED KOCH NEW YORK CITY MAYOR

He should go to a spa and lose some ego.

Bella Abzug

Let him get a job like every other guy....If he doesn't get a job he should retire to Florida.

Jimmy Breslin

Moron.

Donald Trump

C. EVERETT KOOP U.S. SURGEON GENERAL

Why does he look like an admiral? Is he the Admiral of Health?

Frank Zappa

ROBERT E. LEE CONFEDERATE GENERAL

Lee is the only man I know whom I would follow blindfolded.

Stonewall Jackson

ABRAHAM LINCOLN 16TH U.S. PRESIDENT

The President is nothing more than a well-meaning baboon....What a specimen to be at the head of our affairs now!

George McClellan

Lincoln went down in history as "Honest Abe," but he never was a jockey. If he had been a jockey he might have gone down as just "Abe."

Will Rogers

DAVID LLOYD GEORGE BRITISH PRIME MINISTER

Oh, if I could piss the way he speaks!

Georges Clemenceau

HUEY P. LONG LOUISIANA GOVERNOR

He would light on one part of you, sting you, and then when you slapped at him, fly away to land elsewhere and sting again.
Alben Barkley

ALICE ROOSEVELT LONGWORTH SOCIALITE, WIT

I can do one of two things. I can be President of the United States or I can control Alice. I cannot possibly do both.
Theodore Roosevelt

LOUIS XIV FRENCH KING

Strip your Louis Quatorze of his king-gear and there is left nothing but a poor forked radish with a head fantastically carved.
Thomas Carlyle

DOUGLAS MacARTHUR U.S. ARMY GENERAL

I studied dramatics under him for twelve years.
Dwight D. Eisenhower

I didn't fire him because he was a dumb son of a bitch, although he was, but that's not against the law for generals. If it was, half to three-quarters of them would be in jail.   **Harry S Truman**

JAMES MADISON 4TH U.S. PRESIDENT

Oh, poor Jemmy, he is but a withered little applejohn.
Washington Irving

JEB MAGRUDER U.S. POLITICIAN, WATERGATE PARTICIPANT

Jeb, if you don't take your arm off me I'm going to break it off and beat you to death with it.   **G. Gordon Liddy**

NELSON MANDELA SOUTH AFRICAN POLITICIAN, CIVIL RIGHTS ACTIVIST

Nelson Mandela is no Martin Luther King. He is more like H. Rap Brown or Willie Horton.   **William Dannemeyer**

IMELDA MARCOS PHILIPPINE POLITICAL LEADER

Compared to Imelda, Marie Antoinette was a bag lady.
Stephen J. Solarz

PRINCESS MARGARET ROYAL BRIT

[Wears] the kind of styles that make Londoners grateful for their fog!
Mr. (Earl) Blackwell

KARL MARX FOUNDER OF COMMUNISM

The world would not be in such a snarl
Had Marx been Groucho instead of Karl.
Irving Berlin

M is for Marx
And clashing of classes
And movement of masses
And massing of asses.
Cyril Connolly

GEORGE McCLELLAN U.S. ARMY GENERAL, PRESIDENTIAL CANDIDATE

My dear McClellan: If you don't want to use the army I should like to borrow it for a while.
Abraham Lincoln

GEORGE McGOVERN U.S. SENATOR, PRESIDENTIAL CANDIDATE

Talking with George McGovern is like eating a Chinese meal. An hour after it's over you wonder whether you really ate anything.
Eugene McCarthy

So boring he made your skull feel like it was imploding.
Tom Wolfe

WILLIAM McKINLEY 25TH U.S. PRESIDENT

McKinley has a chocolate éclair backbone. **Theodore Roosevelt**

EDWIN MEESE U.S. ATTORNEY GENERAL

The standard for the Attorney General nominee should not be: can he prove he is not a felon?
Senator Joseph Biden

VYACHESLAV MOLOTOV RUSSIAN STATESMAN, DIPLOMAT

He can't even find foreign countries on the map, let alone deal with them.   **Joseph Stalin**

WALTER MONDALE U.S. VICE-PRESIDENT

I was up in New England the other day, campaigning in Vermont, and I said, "It's nice to be here in Vermont when the sap is running," and one of the pickets stood up and said, "Stop talking about Mondale that way."   **George Bush**

Walter Mondale has the charisma of a speed bump.   **Will Durst**

If I had as much make-up on as he did, I'd have looked younger, too.   **Ronald Reagan**

BENITO MUSSOLINI ITALIAN DICTATOR

Il Duce, believing as he does in press censorship, probably will cut the last three words from the headline "Mussolini Best Man at Marconi's Wedding."   **Franklin Pierce Adams**

That loud frogmouth.   **W.C. Fields**

RALPH NADER ATTORNEY, CONSUMER ADVOCATE

When Ralph Nader tells me he wants my car to be cheap, ugly and slow, he's imposing a way of life on me that I'm going to resist to the bitter end.   **Timothy Leary**

NAPOLEON III FRENCH EMPEROR

His mind was a kind of extinct sulphur-pit.   **Thomas Carlyle**

RICHARD NIXON 37TH U.S. PRESIDENT

Nixon is a purposeless man, but I have great faith in his cowardice.   **Jimmy Breslin**

I'm a fan of President Nixon. I worship the quicksand he walks on.   **Art Buchwald**

President Nixon's motto was: if two wrongs don't make a right, try three.   **Norman Cousins**

He is the president of every place in this country which does not have a bookstore.   **Murray Kempton**

Do you realize the responsibility I carry? I'm the only person standing between Nixon and the White House. **John F. Kennedy**

Richard Nixon represents the dark side of the American spirit.
Robert F. Kennedy

The essence of this man is loneliness.   **Henry Kissinger**

I won't go so far as to say he's insane. I will go so far as to say I find his behavior peculiar.   **George McGovern**

As President Nixon says, presidents can do almost anything, and President Nixon has done many things that nobody would have thought of doing.   **Golda Meir**

I used to play poker with him, and any guy who could screech over losing forty bucks I always thought shouldn't be President of the United States.   **Tip O'Neill**

Richard Nixon inherited some good instincts from his Quaker forebears, but by diligent hard work he overcame them.
James Reston

One has the uneasy feeling that he is always on the verge of pronouncing himself the victim of some clandestine plot.
Arthur Schlesinger, Jr.

He is the kind of politician who would cut down a redwood tree, then mount the stump and make a speech for conservation.
Adlai Stevenson

...a shifty-eyed goddamn liar...one of the few in the history of this country to run for high office talking out of both sides of his mouth at the same time and lying out of both sides.   **Harry S Truman**

TRICIA NIXON DAUGHTER OF RICHARD NIXON

The worst thing a little acid could do to Tricia Nixon is turn her into a merely delightful person instead of a grinning robot. **Grace Slick**

JACQUELINE KENNEDY ONASSIS U.S. FIRST LADY, LITERARY EDITOR

She's got to learn to reconcile herself to being Mrs. Aristotle Onassis because the only place she'll find sympathy from now on is in the dictionary between shit and syphilis. **Aristotle Onassis**

Jacqueline Onassis has a very clear understanding of marriage. I have a lot of respect for women who win the game with rules given to you by the enemy. **Gloria Steinem**

THOMAS PAINE U.S. POLITICIAN, PHILOSOPHER

. . .a mongrel between pig and puppy, begotten by a wild boar on a bitch wolf. **John Adams**

That dirty little atheist. **Theodore Roosevelt**

ROSS PEROT U.S. PRESIDENTIAL CANDIDATE, BUSINESS LEADER

. . .a hand grenade with a bad haircut. **Rush Limbaugh**

You can't compete with a pet rock. **Dee Dee Myers**

FRANKLIN PIERCE 14TH U.S. PRESIDENT

Pierce was either the worst or he was the weakest of all our presidents. **Ralph Waldo Emerson**

Pierce didn't know what was going on, and even if he had he wouldn't of known what to do about it. **Harry S Truman**

JAMES KNOX POLK 11TH U.S. PRESIDENT

A victim of the use of water as a beverage. **Sam Houston**

MUAMMAR QADDAFI LIBYAN MILITARY/POLITICAL LEADER

We know that this mad dog of the Middle East has a goal of a world revolution.   **Ronald Reagan**

DAN QUAYLE U.S. VICE-PRESIDENT

I don't like to deal in rumors, but I heard that the guy who took Dan Quayle's law boards for him, *he* cheated.   **Albert Brooks**

Cabin boy.   **Mario Cuomo**

The Secret Service is under orders that if Bush is shot, to shoot Quayle.   **John Kerry**

Dan Quayle deserves to be vice-president like Elvis deserved his black belt in karate.   **Dennis Miller**

Anyone who knows Dan Quayle knows he would rather play golf than have sex any day.   **Marilyn Quayle**

He could pick up his clothes a little more.   **Marilyn Quayle**

An empty suit that goes to funerals and plays golf.   **Ross Perot**

As for the look on Dan Quayle's face—how to describe it? Well, let's see. If a tree fell in a forest and no one was there to hear it, it might sound like Dan Quayle looks.   **Tom Shales**

NANCY REAGAN U.S. FIRST LADY

Nancy Reagan fell down and broke her hair.   **Johnny Carson**

Nancy Reagan has agreed to be the first artificial heart donor.
               Andrea C. Michaels, as quoted by Herb Caen

As a matter of fact, Nancy never had any interest in politics or anything else when we got married.   **Ronald Reagan**

Turkey neck.   **Joan Rivers**

A dope with fat ankles.   **Frank Sinatra**

...projects the passion of a Good Humor ice cream: frozen, on a stick and all vanilla.   **Spencer Tracy**

RONALD REAGAN 40TH U.S. PRESIDENT, GOVERNOR OF CALIFORNIA

Reagan has done the work of two men—Laurel and Hardy.
                                                    Joey Adams

Ronald Reagan's platform seems to be: "Hey, I'm a big good-looking guy and I need a lot of sleep."   **Roy Blount, Jr.**

Reagan's in the news again. He's at his ranch chopping wood—he's building the log cabin he was born in.   **Johnny Carson**

An amiable dunce.   **Clark Clifford**

I'm glad Reagan is president. Of course, I'm a professional comedian.   **Will Durst**

Governor Reagan and I have one thing in common. We both played football....I played for Michigan. He played for Warner Bros.   **Gerald Ford**

Ronald Reagan doesn't dye his hair—he's just prematurely orange.   **Gerald Ford**

The youthful sparkle in Ronald Reagan's eyes is caused by his contact lenses, which he keeps highly polished.   **Sheilah Graham**

I don't wear any more make-up than Reagan.
                                        Pee Wee Herman (Paul Reubens)

Ronald Reagan is not a typical politician because he doesn't know how to lie, cheat and steal. He's always had an agent for that.   **Bob Hope**

He ticks me off. First of all, he's got hair.   **Ed Koch**

I believe that Ronald Reagan can make this country what it once was—an arctic region covered with ice.   **Steve Martin**

You've got to be careful quoting Ronald Reagan because when you quote him accurately it's called mudslinging. **Walter Mondale**

Ronald Reagan is the first president to be accompanied by a Silly Statement Repair Team. **Mark Russell**

Washington couldn't tell a lie, Nixon couldn't tell the truth, and Reagan couldn't tell the difference. **Mort Sahl**

Reagan won because he ran against Jimmy Carter. Had he run unopposed he would have lost. **Mort Sahl**

Sometimes I think America likes Reagan but they're a little disappointed that they couldn't get Jimmy Stewart. **Ian Shoales**

You know, it's a pity about Ronnie—he doesn't understand economics at all. **Margaret Thatcher**

A triumph of the embalmer's art. **Gore Vidal**

There's a lot to be said for being *nouveau riche* and the Reagans mean to say it all. **Gore Vidal**

No, no, no, no. You've got it all wrong. Jimmy Stewart for governor, Ronald Reagan for best friend. **Jack L. Warner**

I still think Nancy does most of his talking; you'll notice that she *never* drinks water when Ronnie speaks. **Robin Williams**

ELEANOR ROOSEVELT U.S. FIRST LADY

She hated my father and she can't stand it that his children turned out so much better than hers. **John F. Kennedy**

Eleanor is a Trojan mare. **Alice Roosevelt Longworth**

No woman has ever so comforted the distressed or so distressed the comfortable. **Clare Booth Luce**

FRANKLIN ROOSEVELT 32ND U.S. PRESIDENT

If Roosevelt were alive today he'd turn over in his grave.
Samuel Goldwyn

A chameleon on plaid.   **Herbert Hoover**

One-third Eleanor and two-thirds mush.
                              Alice Roosevelt Longworth

The croon of croons.   **H.L. Mencken**

If he became convinced tomorrow that coming out for cannibalism would get him the votes he so sorely needs, he would begin fattening a missionary on the White House backyard come Wednesday.   **H.L. Mencken**

The Rotarian to end all Rotarians.   **Malcolm Muggeridge**

Franklin Roosevelt was a lousy student. He failed the bar exam seven times.   **Marilyn Quayle**

THEODORE ROOSEVELT 26TH U.S. PRESIDENT

He played all his cards—if not more.   **Oliver Wendell Holmes**

I have always found Roosevelt an amusing fellow, but I would not employ him, except for reasons of personal friendship, as a geek in a common carnival.   **Murray Kempton**

He hated all pretension save his own pretension.   **H.L. Mencken**

When Theodore attends a wedding he wants to be the bride, and when he attends a funeral he wants to be the corpse.
                              Alice Roosevelt Longworth

His idea of getting hold of the right end of the stick is to snatch it from the hands of somebody who is using it effectively and hit him over the head with it.   **George Bernard Shaw**

Roosevelt bit me and I went mad.   **William Allen White**

PHYLLIS SCHLAFLY ANTI-FEMINIST WRITER, U.S. POLITICIAN

Phyllis Schlafly should be tied up and forced to watch people minding their own business.   **Elayne Boosler**

Phyllis Schlafly speaks for all American women who oppose equal rights for themselves.
Andy Rooney

GEORGE SHULTZ U.S. STATESMAN

The reason that poor Shultz is getting the reputation of a dull plodder...is that the right-wing wackos around the administration keep going behind his back and accusing him of overt sanity.
Calvin Trillin

F.E. (FREDERICK EDWIN) SMITH BRITISH POLITICIAN

Very clever, but his brains go to his head.
Margot Asquith

ANASTASIO SOMOZA NICARAGUAN PRESIDENT

He may be a son of a bitch, but he's our son of a bitch.
Franklin Roosevelt

JOSEPH STALIN RUSSIAN POLITICAL LEADER

There are still some people who think that we have Stalin to thank for all our progress, who quake before Stalin's dirty underdrawers, who stand at attention and salute them.
Nikita Khrushchev

He rolled the executions on his tongue like berries.
Osip Mandelstam

I like old Joe Stalin.
Harry S Truman

ADLAI STEVENSON U.S. POLITICIAN, PRESIDENTIAL CANDIDATE

Adlai the appeaser...who got his Ph.D. from Dean Acheson's College of Cowardly Communist Containment.
Richard Nixon

My God, in this job he's got the nerve of a burglar.
John F. Kennedy

The real trouble with Stevenson is that he's no better than a regular sissy.
Harry S Truman

JOHN SUNUNU U.S. POLITICIAN

I won't say he flew a lot. But he won't start a cabinet meeting until the seat backs and tray tables are locked into the upright position. **Robert Dole**

What do you do if you're in a room with Muammar Qaddafi, Saddam Hussein and John Sununu and you have a gun that has only two bullets? Shoot Sununu twice. **Michael Dukakis**

WILLIAM HOWARD TAFT 27TH U.S. PRESIDENT

The Great Postponer. **William Jennings Bryan**

He looked at me as if I was a side dish he hadn't ordered.
Ring Lardner

CHARLES-MAURICE DE TALLEYRAND
FRENCH STATESMAN, DIPLOMAT

He is a silk stocking filled with dung. **Napoleon Bonaparte**

ZACHARY TAYLOR 12TH U.S. PRESIDENT

Few men have ever had a more comfortable, labor-saving contempt for learning of every kind. **Winfield Scott**

MARGARET THATCHER BRITISH PRIME MINISTER

She approaches the problems of our country with all the one-dimensional subtlety of a comic strip. **Dennis Healy**

Mrs. Thatcher...has guts and all that, and she's pretty intelligent.
Mick Jagger

She only went to Venice because somebody told her she could walk down the middle of the street. **Neil Kinnock**

When I hear the Prime Minister feeling sorry for the rest of the world, I understand why she has taken to calling herself "we"—it is less lonely. **Neil Kinnock**

She has eyes like Caligula and the mouth of Marilyn Monroe.

François Mitterrand

She's the best man in England. **Ronald Reagan**

If I were married to her I'd be sure to have dinner ready when she got home. **George Shultz**

PIERRE TRUDEAU CANADIAN PRIME MINISTER

In Pierre Elliot Trudeau Canada has at last produced a political leader worthy of assassination. **Irving Layton**

That asshole. **Richard Nixon**

HARRY S TRUMAN 33RD U.S. PRESIDENT

...grew up so poor that his family could not afford to put a period after his middle initial. **Dave Barry**

Mr. Truman believes other people should be "free to govern themselves as they see fit"—so long as they see fit to see as we see fit. **I.F. Stone**

VICTORIA BRITISH QUEEN (1837–1901)

She's more of a man than I expected. **Henry James**

Nowadays, a parlor maid as ignorant as Queen Victoria was when she came to the throne would be classed as mentally defective. **George Bernard Shaw**

GEORGE WALLACE
U.S. PRESIDENTIAL CANDIDATE, GOVERNOR OF ALABAMA

I'd dig to meet Wallace. The governor. Yeah, I bet he's a gas, man, behind his game. **Keith Richards**

HENRY WALLACE U.S. VICE-PRESIDENT

Much of what Mr. Wallace calls his global thinking is, no matter how you slice it, still Globaloney. **Clare Booth Luce**

GEORGE WASHINGTON 1ST U.S. PRESIDENT

Did anyone ever see Washington nude? It is inconceivable. He had no nakedness, but I imagine he was born with his clothes on and his hair powdered, and made a stately bow on his first appearance in the world. **Nathaniel Hawthorne**

He was ignorant of the commonest accomplishments of youth. He could not even lie. **Mark Twain**

DANIEL WEBSTER U.S. SECRETARY OF STATE

...the gigantic intellect, the envious temper, the ravenous ambition and the rotten heart of Daniel Webster. **John Quincy Adams**

The word *honor* in the mouth of Mr. Webster is like the word *love* in the mouth of a whore. **Ralph Waldo Emerson**

CASPAR WEINBERGER U.S. DEFENSE SECRETARY

He's lost all credibility. Instead of Cap the Knife, he's Cap the Ladle. **Al Gore**

WILLIAM IV BRITISH KING

The King blew his nose twice and wiped the royal perspiration repeatedly from a face which is probably the largest uncivilized spot in England. **Oliver Wendell Holmes**

WOODROW WILSON 28TH U.S. PRESIDENT

Mr. Wilson's mind, as has been the custom, will be closed all day Sunday. **George S. Kaufman**

Like Odysseus, he looked wiser when seated.
John Maynard Keynes

A Byzantine logothete. **Theodore Roosevelt**

BAD SPORTS

"Generally speaking, I look upon sports as
dangerous and tiring activities performed by
people with whom I share nothing except
the right to trial by jury."

FRAN LEBOWITZ

HANK AARON BASEBALL'S "HAMMERIN' HANK"

The only man I idolize more than myself is Henry Aaron.

Muhammad Ali

DANNY AINGE BASKETBALL PLAYER

Ainge hurt his back picking up a suitcase. It must have had his contract in it.

Dick Motta

MUHAMMAD ALI "THE GREATEST" BOXER

I've never seen him in anything, but I suspect that he shouldn't be acting and that's why I never bothered.

Jim Murray

MIKE ANDERSON OUTFIELDER, PHILADELPHIA PHILLIES

Mike Anderson's limitations are limitless.

Danny Ozark

SPARKY ANDERSON
BASEBALL MANAGER KNOWN AS "CAPTAIN HOOK"

Sparky came here two years ago promising to build a team in his own image, and now the club is looking for small, white-haired infielders with .212 batting averages.

Al Ackerman

RED AUERBACH BASKETBALL COACH, BOSTON CELTICS

I always thought that Red would be the type of guy who if he was standing on the street corner and some kid came up to him for an autograph, he'd say, "Who asked you to come over here?"

Paul Seymour

CHARLES BARKLEY BASKETBALL'S "SIR CHARLES"

He's so fat that his bathtub has stretch marks.

Pat Williams

FRANCISCO BARRIOS BASEBALL PITCHER

He threw good, but he's still ugly. He scares the ball to the plate. It'll do anything to get away from him.

Jim Morrison

GREG BINGHAM FOOTBALL PLAYER

To keep Greg Bingham out of a game you'd have to cut off his head and then hide it. Just cuttin' off his head wouldn't accomplish anything. He'd find it and try to play anyway.

Bum Phillips

MANUTE BOL BASKETBALL PLAYER

He's so thin the '76ers don't bother to take him on the road— they just fax him from town to town. **Woody Allen**

He's so skinny his pajamas have only one pinstripe.

Pat Williams

He looks like he went to the bloodbank and forgot to say when.

Pat Williams

BRIAN BOSWORTH FOOTBALL'S "BOZ"

He's got a gimmick, though, and everybody loves it. They're paying to see his hair. **Art Donovan**

He is the only football player in history to make more deodorant commercials than tackles. **Scott Ostler**

TERRY BRADSHAW FOOTBALL'S "OZARK IKE"

Terry Bradshaw couldn't spell cat if you spotted him the C and the A. **Thomas Henderson**

JIM BROWN FOOTBALL GREAT

Every time I tackle Jim Brown I hear a dice game going on inside my mouth. **Don Burroughs**

LEW BURDETTE BASEBALL PITCHER

Lew Burdette would make coffee nervous. **Fred Haney**

JOSÉ CANSECO BASEBALL PLAYER

The best thing about him is that he's built like a Greek goddess.

Sparky Anderson

WILT CHAMBERLAIN BASKETBALL'S "BIG DIPPER"

He says he slept with twenty thousand women and everyone thinks that's funny. If a woman had done that...I mean, why didn't someone just say to him, "You're a disgusting pig"?

Robin Givens

Wilt Chamberlain says his New Year's resolution is to stop fooling around so much. He wants to find the right two or three hundred women and settle down.

Jay Leno

Sir Edmund Hillary was introduced to Wilt and promptly organized an expedition to climb it.

Jim Murray

HAPPY CHANDLER BASEBALL COMMISSIONER

Happy left office for reasons of health; that is, the owners got sick of him.

Red Smith

HAL CHASE BASEBALL'S "PEERLESS HAL"

He had a corkscrew brain.

Jim Price

TY COBB BASEBALL'S "GEORGIA GHOST"

He would climb a mountain to take a punch at an echo.

Arthur "Bugs" Baer

Cobb is a prick. But he can hit. God almighty, that man can hit.

Babe Ruth

HOWARD COSELL SPORTS COMMENTATOR

Sometimes Howard makes me wish I was a dog and he was a fireplug.

Muhammad Ali

He's a tremendous ham, a cartoonlike character. He comes across that way on TV, too. He's the same way if you're eating dinner with him—he broadcasts the meal.

Woody Allen

Why are we honoring this man? Have we run out of human beings?

Milton Berle

He once walked around with a harpoon sticking out of him for two weeks without noticing it.

Dick Cavett

If you split this guy open, demons and poison would spill all over the floor.   **Bob Costas**

Color me skeptical of the rumor that Howard Cosell was abandoned by wolves and raised by his parents.   **Larry Guest**

There have always been mixed emotions about Howard Cosell. Some people hate him like poison and some people just hate him regular.   **Buddy Hackett**

More than anyone I know, he sucks the oxygen out of a room.
David Halberstam

In the next issue of *Cosmopolitan* Howard Cosell will be the centerfold with his vital organ covered—his mouth.   **Burt Reynolds**

...published a 390-page autobiography in 1973 in which he did not once mention his mother's name.   **Liz Smith**

The Russians have a weapon that can wipe out 280 million Americans. That puts them exactly ten years behind Howard Cosell.   **Red Smith**

In one year I traveled 450,000 miles by air. That's 18-1/2 times around the world or once around Howard Cosell's head.
Jackie Stewart

BILL CURRY   COLLEGE FOOTBALL COACH

Getting replaced by Bill Curry, that really bothered me. It's kind of like having your wife run off with Don Knotts.

Pepper Rodgers

AL DAVIS   OWNER, OAKLAND RAIDERS

Dislike? Hell, I hate the son of a bitch!   **Gene Klein**

RON DIBBLE   BASEBALL PITCHER

Give him a couple of million. He shouldn't have to take a second job to support himself or anything.   **José Canseco**

MIKE DITKA   FOOTBALL'S "HAMMER"

Mike Ditka is a fatheaded redneck.   **James Brooks**

He reminds me of many of the coaches back in the NFL of the 1950s: fascist, loud…not exactly Phi Beta Kappa. **Jim Brown**

If I were the NFL commissioner I'd put all the offensive linemen in jail for thirty days or make them spend one week with Mike Ditka. **Dexter Manley**

ABNER DOUBLEDAY BASEBALL INVENTOR

Errors are part of the game, but Abner Doubleday was a jerk for inventing them. **Billy Ripken**

DON DRYSDALE SPITBALLER

He talks very well for a guy who's had two fingers in his mouth all his life. **Gene Mauch**

LEO DUROCHER BASEBALL'S "LIP"

Leo Durocher is a man with an infinite capacity to take a bad situation and make it immediately worse. **Branch Rickey**

NICK ETTEN BASEBALL PLAYER

Nick Etten's glove fields better with Nick Etten out of it.
Joe Trimble

CHARLES O. FINLEY OWNER, OAKLAND A'S BASEBALL TEAM

Finley treated me like a colored boy. **Vida Blue**

Charlie Finley wouldn't think God would make a good commissioner. **Warren Giles**

We had a common bond on the A's: everybody hated Charlie Finley. **Reggie Jackson**

When Charlie had his heart operation it took eight hours—seven-and-a-half just to find his heart. **Steve McCatty**

Finley is a self-made man who worships his creator. **Jim Murray**

DOUG FLUTIE FOOTBALL PLAYER

Bambi, America's favorite midget. **Jim McMahon**

JIMMIE FOXX BASEBALL'S "DOUBLE X"

Jimmie Foxx wasn't scouted—he was trapped. **Lefty Gomez**

He has muscles in his hair. **Lefty Gomez**

MIKE FRATELLO BASKETBALL COACH

…Mike Fratello, who is trying to ruin the English language by saying *elevate* when he means *jump*. Mike! Go elevate in a lake.

Scott Ostler

JIM FREY BASEBALL MANAGER

Jim Frey has the emotional intensity of a comatose eggplant.

Bill James

If it's true that we learn by our mistakes, then Jim Frey will be the best manager ever. **Ron Luciano**

JOE GARAGIOLA SPORTSCASTER

Hey Joe, is that sunroof standard equipment on that body?

Bill Madlock

Joe Garagiola is an inspiration to young athletes everywhere. I've never seen this man with a drink, a cigarette or a comb.

Dean Martin

STEVE GARVEY BASEBALL PLAYER

There's been some speculation he might sign with the Yankees. This would be like Donny Osmond joining the PLO.

Johnny Carson

Anyone who has plastic hair is bound to have problems.

Jay Johnstone

He wears sunglasses when he goes to X-rated movies.

Tommy Lasorda

He's so goody, he goes out behind the barn to chew gum.

Don Rickles

CHARLIE GEHRINGER BASEBALL'S "MECHANICAL MAN"

Charlie Gehringer is in a rut. He bats .350 on opening day and stays there all season. **Lefty Gomez**

BOB GIBSON BASEBALL'S "OLD MASTER"

Gibson's the luckiest pitcher I've ever seen because he always picks the night to pitch when the other team doesn't score any runs. **Tim McCarver**

FRANK GIFFORD FOOTBALL PLAYER, SPORTSCASTER

I turn my back for two and a half hours...I look up. [Kathie Lee] has him out the checkout counter, out the door, bagged and in her car....I didn't even know what hit me. **Diane Sawyer**

JERRY GLANVILLE FOOTBALL COACH

Drop me a note if you find somebody who likes this guy, will you? **Sam Wyche**

GOOSE GOSSAGE BASEBALL'S "WHITE GORILLA"

The Goose should do more pitching and less quacking. **George Steinbrenner**

RED GRANGE FOOTBALL'S "GALLOPING GHOST"

Three or four men and a horse rolled into one. **Damon Runyon**

"MEAN" JOE GREEN FOOTBALL PLAYER

Joe Greene was on "Wild Kingdom" once and they shot him. **Don Rickles**

LEFTY GROVE BASEBALL PITCHER

He could throw a lamb chop past a wolf. **Westbrook Pegler**

He was a moody guy, a tantrum thrower like me, but when he punched a locker or something he always did it with his right hand. He was a careful tantrum thrower.   **Ted Williams**

MARVIN HAGLER "MARVELOUS" BOXER

Hagler uses his bald head as a third hand. I'm a far cleaner fighter. He should be grateful I'm making him so much money. He would not get ten million bucks for fighting anyone else.

Roberto Duran

GEORGE HALAS OWNER, CHICAGO BEARS FOOTBALL TEAM

He throws around nickels like they were manhole covers.

Mike Ditka

TIM HARRIS FOOTBALL PLAYER

Sometimes God gives out all the physical talent and takes away the brain.   **Mike Ditka**

MICKEY HATCHER BASEBALL PLAYER

He's the first guy ever to make the majors on one brain cell.

Roy Smalley

VON HAYES BASEBALL STAR

He looks like a pair of pliers.   **Johnny Bench**

ELROY HIRSCH FOOTBALL'S "CRAZYLEGS"

You've heard of people who zig or zag. Well, Elroy also had a zog and a couple of zugs.   **Norm Van Brocklin**

HULK HOGAN WRESTLER, ACTOR

I don't know what it is, but I can't look at Hulk Hogan and believe that he's the end result of millions and millions of years of evolution.   **Jim Murray**

MIKE HOLOVAK | MANAGER, HOUSTON OILERS FOOTBALL TEAM

I don't know why we didn't get along. Most dead people like me.

Jerry Glanville

CARL HUBBELL | BASEBALL'S "MEAL TICKET"

The only eccentric thing about him is his crooked arm. He looks as if he put it on in the dark.

Jim Murray

REGGIE JACKSON | BASEBALL'S "MR. OCTOBER"

The only thing Reggie can do better than me on the field is talk.

Rod Carew

When you unwrap a Reggie bar it tells you how good it is.

Catfish Hunter

He'd give you the shirt off of his back. Of course, he'd call a press conference to announce it.

Catfish Hunter

Reggie once said that the only people he can relate to are the writers. That's because they are the only ones who benefit from hearing his crap.

Sparky Lyle

If his hair gets any longer he'll need a ladder to put his hat on. If Reggie got a haircut he'd be a midget.

Don Rickles

Reggie's got an IQ of 160? Out of what—a thousand?

Mickey Rivers

If a person can't hate Reggie Jackson, who can he hate?

Mike Royko

When a streak hitter like Reggie Jackson can get a candy bar named after him, you conclude that the word *superstar* has been devalued. Or even the word *candy bar*.

Bob Uecker

TOMMY JOHN | BASEBALL PITCHER

Ask him for the time and he'll tell you how to make a watch.

Bob Lemon

CLIFF JOHNSON | BASEBALL PLAYER

He's so ugly he should have to wear an oxygen mask.

Mickey Rivers

Johnson just washed his legs today and can't do a thing with them.   **Lon Simmons**

JIMMY JOHNSON   FOOTBALL COACH

If he wanted me to run twenty-six miles through hills, I would. If he wanted me to carry water bottles, I would. If he wanted me to go to the barber and get my hair cut like his...well, you have to draw the line somewhere.   **Babe Laufenberg**

The only time Jimmy didn't run up a score was twenty-seven years ago when he took the SAT.   **Jim Nantz**

MICHAEL JORDAN   BASKETBALL'S "AIR JORDAN"

When you're playing him you try to talk about things Michael doesn't like to talk about. Like baldness.   **John Salley**

KEN KAISER   BASEBALL UMPIRE

Dr. Strangecall.   **Whitey Herzog**

DON KING   BOXING PROMOTER

One day Don King will asphyxiate by the force of his own exhaust.   **Carmen Graciano**

Don King doesn't care about black or white. He just cares about green.   **Larry Holmes**

BILL KLEM   BASEBALL UMP, "THE OLD ARBITRATOR"

I just thought you might like to know that I passed a kennel on the way to the game and your mother is all right.   **Ralph Houk**

BOBBY KNIGHT   BASKETBALL COACH, INDIANA UNIVERSITY

Bobby Knight is a good friend of mine. But if I ever need a heart transplant, I want his. It's never been used.   **George Raveling**

HARVEY KUENN   BASEBALL MANAGER

Harvey Kuenn's face looks as if it could hold three days of rain.
                                                        Tommy Lasorda

BOWIE KUHN BASEBALL COMMISSIONER

If I hear him say just once more he's doing something for the betterment of baseball, I'm going to throw up.   **Sparky Anderson**

If Bowie Kuhn had a brain in his head, he'd be an idiot.
Charles O. Finley

Bowie Kuhn is the biggest jerk in the history of baseball.
Charles O. Finley

Other than a tack on his seat, nothing could make Kuhn jump faster than when he saw a television camera.   **Red Smith**

BILL LAIMBEER BASKETBALL PLAYER, LAKERS

A 6'10" white guy who can't jump over a piece of paper.
Charles Barkley

Bill Laimbeer is not a candidate for the basketball Hall of Fame unless the Hall adds a jerk wing.   **Jan Hubbard**

I assume his parents like him. But you'd have to verify that.
Kurt Rambis

KENESAW MOUNTAIN LANDIS BASEBALL COMMISSIONER

His career typifies the heights to which dramatic talent may carry a man in America if only he has the foresight not to go on the stage.   **Heywood Broun**

He didn't know a baseball from a bale of hay.   **Happy Chandler**

TOM LANDRY FOOTBALL'S "ICEBERG"

Don't read Landry's playbook all the way through. Everybody dies at the end.   **Peter Gent**

He's such a perfectionist that if he were married to Dolly Parton he'd expect her to cook.   **Don Meredith**

TOMMY LASORDA BASEBALL PLAYER, MANAGER

You can plant two thousand rows of corn with the fertilizer Lasorda spreads around.   **Joe Garagiola**

Lasorda's standard reply when some new kid would ask directions to the whirlpool was to tell him to stick his foot in the toilet and flush it. **Steve Garvey**

If anyone could make sparks fly off a plastic fork, Lasorda is the man. **Scott Ostler**

Did you hear what happened? Tommy was lying on the beach in Santa Monica and Greenpeace tried to roll him back in the water. **Steve Sax**

We're given a choice: we can either run around the field three times or around Tommy Lasorda once. **Steve Sax**

Every year Tommy offers $50,000 to the family of the unknown soldier. **Don Sutton**

VINCE LOMBARDI FOOTBALL COACH

Coach Lombardi is very fair. He treats us all like dogs.
Henry Jordan

GREG LUZINSKI BASEBALL'S "BULL"

If you took those two legs and barbecued them, you'd have enough to feed a family for a month. **Larry Bowa**

SAL MAGLIE BASEBALL'S "BARBER"

He's got those big evil-looking black eyes. Looks something like Snoopy doing the vulture bit. **Jim Bouton**

KARL MALONE BASKETBALL'S "MAILMAN"

Karl Malone's basketball trunks are as roomy as jammies. They ought to have Ninja Turtle decals on them. **Mike Downey**

MICKEY MANTLE BASEBALL'S "COMMERCE COMET"

Mickey Mantle can hit just as good right-handed as he can left-handed. He's just naturally amphibious. **Yogi Berra**

Everybody who roomed with Mickey said he took five years off their career. **Whitey Ford**

Mantle burped at the fans until he lived to be fifty and needed to become a grand old guy.   **George Vecsey**

BILLY MARTIN BASEBALL'S "GREAT AGITATOR"

Lots of people look up to Billy Martin. That's because he's just knocked them down.   **Jim Bouton**

Today is opening day in baseball. Out in Yankee Stadium Billy Martin threw out the first punch.   **Johnny Carson**

Billy is starting to lose his cool. Today he pistol-whipped a pay toilet.   **Johnny Carson**

"Billy Ball" is a system of play where you fight your own players, the others' players, the umpires, owners, press and strangers in a bar, and then when you win and someone wants to know the secret you say, "Teamwork."   **Nestor Chylak**

When Billy Martin reaches for a bar tab, his arm shrinks six inches.   **Tommy Lasorda**

Some people have a chip on their shoulder. Billy has a whole lumberyard.   **Jim Murray**

GENE MAUCH BASEBALL'S "LITTLE GENERAL"

Gene Mauch's stare can put you on the disabled list.

Tim McCarver

JOHN MAYBERRY BASEBALL PLAYER

He's so slow that you could take sequence photos of him with a Polaroid camera.   **Ron Luciano**

WILLIE MAYS BASEBALL'S "SAY HEY KID "

I never saw a fucking ball go out of a fucking park so fucking fast in my fucking life.   **Leo Durocher**

The last time Willie Mays dropped a pop fly he had a rattle in one hand and a bonnet on his head.   **Jim Murray**

JOHN McENROE TENNIS'S "SUPERBRAT"

McEnroe was charming as always, which means that he was as charming as a dead mouse in a loaf of bread.   **Clive James**

I felt I had the most interesting of all the tennis players—or else it would have been really boring.   **Tatum O'Neal**

DENNY McLAIN BASEBALL'S "SKY KING"

Denny used to be barrel-chested, but the staves have slipped.

Tom Collins

JIM McMAHON FOOTBALL PLAYER

We had a strange and wonderful relationship. He's strange and I'm wonderful.   **Mike Ditka**

AL MICHAELS SPORTSCASTER

Al is inquisitive, knowledgeable and incredibly well-prepared. I don't know what his IQ is, but it's probably only a couple of points lower than mine.   **Dan Dierdorf**

OLIVER MILLER BASKETBALL PLAYER

You can't even jump high enough to touch the rim unless they put a Big Mac on it.   **Charles Barkley**

KEVIN MITCHELL BASEBALL PLAYER

He's the only guy I know who does his clothes shopping at the San Diego Zoo. He puts five animals in the endangered species list with one outfit.   **Bob Brenly**

MANNY MOTA BASEBALL PLAYER

Manny Mota is older than dirt.   **Tommy Lasorda**

VAN LINGLE MUNGO BASEBALL PLAYER

Van Mungo likes to drink a bit. Anything. Even hair tonic.

Leo Durocher

DALE MURPHY BASEBALL PLAYER

I've seen him order everything on the menu except "Thank you for dining with us." **Jerry Royster**

JOE NAMATH FOOTBALL'S "BROADWAY JOE"

The Joe Namaths of the world are meaningless. They come and go, fleeting figures of passing glamour. **Howard Cosell**

I spent twelve years training for a career that was over in a week. Joe Namath spent one week training for a career that lasted twelve years. **Bruce Jenner**

He has great respect for girls. Only last week in New York he saved a girl from being attacked. He controlled himself. **Dean Martin**

I like Joe and he's done okay, but an actor he ain't. But he sure can sell pantyhose and cologne. **Jim Murray**

DANNY NAPOLEON BASEBALL PLAYER

He's so ugly that when a fly ball was hit toward him it would curve away from him. **Mickey Rivers**

He'll be okay if he keeps his hand out of his shirt. **Casey Stengel**

MARTINA NAVRATILOVA TENNIS PLAYER

Martina was so far in the closet she was in danger of being a garment bag. **Rita Mae Brown**

She was beside herself—which, come to think of it, would make a great doubles team. **Scott Ostler**

JACK NICKLAUS GOLF'S "GOLDEN BEAR"

When Jack Nicklaus plays well, he wins. When he plays badly, he finishes second. When he plays terrible, he finishes third.

Johnny Miller

Jack has become a legend in his spare time.   **Chi Chi Rodriguez**

WALTER O'MALLEY BASEBALL EXECUTIVE

There's nothing in the world I wouldn't do for Walter O'Malley. There's nothing he wouldn't do for me. That's the way it is—we go through life doing nothing for each other.   **Gene Autry**

LESLIE O'NEAL FOOTBALL PLAYER

He brings a Louis Vuitton briefcase with him to the locker room. Looks good, but there's nothing in it except maybe his own football cards.   **Burt Grossman**

SHAQUILLE O'NEAL BASKETBALL PLAYER

Shaq's house is in such a great neighborhood the bird feeders have salad bars.   **Pat Williams**

ARNOLD PALMER GOLF'S "CHARGER"

Arnold Palmer is the biggest crowd pleaser since the invention of the portable sanitary facility.   **Bob Hope**

FREDDIE PATEK BASEBALL'S "FLYING FLEA"

Fred Patek was so small when he was born that his father passed out cigar butts.   **Joey Adams**

Freddie Patek is the only guy in the major leagues who needs a life preserver to go into the whirlpool bath. After a game he has to leap to reach the shower knobs.   **Jim Murray**

WILLIAM PERRY FOOTBALL'S "REFRIGERATOR"

Supposedly he weights 325. Hey, who knows? He's running twice a day—from the refrigerator to the bathroom.   **Mike Ditka**

DIGGER PHELPS BASKETBALL COACH, NOTRE DAME

He's a phony, lying, plastic, chickenshit asshole.   **Brad Duggan**

LOU PINIELLA BASEBALL'S "SWEET LOU"

Lou Piniella only argues on days ending with the letter Y.

Ron Luciano

Sweet refers to his swing, not his personality.   **Phil Rizzuto**

GARY PLAYER GOLF GREAT

Gary Player is all right if you like to see a grown man dressed up like Black Bart all the time.   **Don Rickles**

LUIS POLONIA BASEBALL PLAYER

If you hit Polonia 100 fly balls, you could make a movie out of it—*Catch 22*.   **Dennis Lamp**

DOUG RADER BASEBALL MANAGER

When I played for Doug Rader we weren't allowed to leave the clubhouse until all the beer was gone.   **Tim Flannery**

AHMAD RASHAD SPORTSCASTER

We've got the picture—you lift weights with Michael Jordan, you play hoops with him, you hang with him. He probably autographed the Michael Jordan growth-chart poster on your living room wall. You and Air are pals. We believe. Let's move on to other scoops.   **Scott Ostler**

BRANCH RICKEY BASEBALL'S "MAHATMA"

Rickey had both money and players. He just didn't like to see the two of them mix.   **Chuck Connors**

BOBBY RIGGS TENNIS'S "HAPPY HUSTLER"

...a face like Bugs Bunny.   **Jimmy the Greek**

Forty years ago women were playing tennis in floppy hats and funny dresses. Now Bobby Riggs is doing it.   **Billie Jean King**

MICKEY RIVERS BASEBALL'S "MICKEY MOUTH"

You're so dumb you don't even know how to spell IQ.

Carlos May

Mickey Rivers could lift weights all day every day and his throws still wouldn't bruise a baby's lips.   **Doug Rader**

STANLEY ROBERTS BASKETBALL PLAYER

I can't use those fat jokes anymore—Stanley has turned over a new chin.   **Pat Williams**

McDonald's and Wendy's are suing Stanley for non-support.

Pat Williams

JACKIE ROBINSON BASEBALL'S "FIRST"

He was a hard out.   **Yogi Berra**

SUGAR RAY ROBINSON BOXER

I fought Sugar Ray Robinson so many times it's a wonder I didn't get diabetes.   **Jake LaMotta**

PETE ROSE BASEBALL'S "CHARLIE HUSTLE"

He's got a square jaw and a square head, and both match his personality.   **Johnny Bench**

If Pete Rose bets on prison softball games, will he be barred from jail for life?   **Jay Leno**

Pete Rose, playing for his prison's softball team, deliberately gets into an argument with the umpire and gets thrown out of prison.

David Letterman

Pete doesn't count his money anymore, he weighs it. **Stan Musial**

You have to give Pete credit for what he's accomplished. He never went to college and the only book he ever read was *The Pete Rose Story*.   **Karolyn Rose**

CARROLL ROSENBLOOM OWNER, BOSTON COLTS

If you didn't have any tickets to give away, you wouldn't have any friends.   **John Mackey**

BABE RUTH BASEBALL'S "SULTAN OF SWAT"

What a guy—egg-shaped and boisterous, a connoisseur of booze, food and dames.   **Jack Dempsey**

God dressed in a camel's hair polo coat and flat camel's hair cap, God with a flat nose and little piggy eyes, a big grin and a fat black cigar sticking out of the side of it.   **Paul Gallico**

If you cut that big slob in half, most of the concessions at Yankee Stadium would come pouring out.   **Waite Hoyt**

Who is this Baby Ruth? And what does she do?

George Bernard Shaw

BUDDY RYAN FOOTBALL COACH

They [the Philadelphia Eagles] think they can come in here and talk their way into a game. They got that from their coach, the fat man.   **Mike Ditka**

NOLAN RYAN BASEBALL'S "RYAN EXPRESS"

Nolan Ryan is pitching much better now that he has his curve ball straightened out.   **Joe Garagiola**

I love it when I hear the media describe someone forty-four years of age as mature and well-seasoned.   **Dan Quayle**

DON SHULA FOOTBALL COACH

If a nuclear bomb ever dropped on this country, the only things I'm certain will survive are AstroTurf and Don Shula.

Bubba Smith

OZZIE SMITH BASEBALL'S "WIZARD OF OZ"

He plays like he's on a minitrampoline out there, or wearing helium kangaroo shorts maybe.   **Andy Van Slyke**

GEORGE STEINBRENNER BASEBALL'S "PATTON IN PINSTRIPES"

Seeing how none of us ever worked for Genghis Khan, how does it feel to work for George Steinbrenner?　　　**Ted Dawson**

He really should stick to horses. At least he can shoot them if they spit the bit.　　　**Reggie Jackson**

The more we lose, the more he'll fly in. And the more he flies in, the better the chance there'll be a plane crash.　　　**Graig Nettles**

I know how to tell when George Steinbrenner is lying. His lips move.　　　**Jerry Reinsdorf**

Every time you go into his office he greets you warmly and shakes you by the throat.　　　**Al Rosen**

CASEY STENGEL BASEBALL'S "OLD PROFESSOR"

Everybody knows that Casey Stengel has forgotten more baseball than I'll ever know. That's the trouble—he's forgotten it.
　　　Jimmy Piersall

His legs were so lumpy it looked as though he were smuggling walnuts in his stockings.　　　**Bob Uecker**

DAVID STERN NBA COMMISSIONER

David's son asked him to buy him a chemistry set, so David went out and bought DuPont.　　　**Pat Williams**

David is now buying a house in a neighborhood where kids play Little League polo and the Salvation Army band has a string section.　　　**Pat Williams**

CHUCK TANNER BASEBALL MANAGER

Chuck Tanner is the eternal optimist. If he were captain on the Titanic he probably would've said, "Don't worry, folks, we're just going to pick up a little ice and we'll be on our way again."
　　　Joe Garagiola

When I first became a manager I asked Chuck for advice. He told me, "Always rent."　　　**Tony LaRussa**

MARV THRONEBERRY   BASEBALL PLAYER

Having Marv Throneberry play for your team is like having
Willie Sutton play for your bank.   **Jimmy Breslin**

We were going to get a birthday cake but we figured you'd drop it.
Casey Stengel

MIKE TYSON   BOXING'S "IRON MIKE"

He's not all that bad. If you dig deep, dig real deep, dig, dig, dig,
dig deep, deep, go all the way to China, I'm sure you'll find
there's a nice guy there.   **George Foreman**

FERNANDO VALENZUELA   BASEBALL'S "TORTILLA FLATS"

Fernando Valenzuela now makes one million dollars a year.
Three years ago Valenzuela's alarm clock was a rooster.
Tommy Lasorda

DICK WILLIAMS   BASEBALL MANAGER

I like playing for Dick, but once I get out of the game I'm going to
run over him with a car.   **Tim Flannery**

MAURY WILLS   BASEBALL MANAGER

Managing is a low-security profession, as I was saying on my way
over here to my cab driver Maury Wills.   **Lindsay Nelson**

RICH YETT   BASEBALL PITCHER

I thought he'd been at the beach all summer—he still had his
inner tube around his stomach.   **Billy Gardner**

DON ZIMMER   BASEBALL'S "BUFFALO HEAD"

That face—it looks like a blocked kick.   **Joe Garagiola**

The designated gerbil.   **Bill Lee**

I've reserved three seats for you at my show tonight. One for you,
one for your wife and one for your stomach.   **Don Rickles**

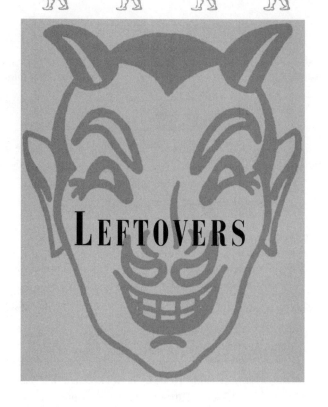

LEFTOVERS

"Critics? I love every bone in their heads."

EUGENE O'NEAL

CHARLES ADDAMS CARTOONIST, "THE ADDAMS FAMILY"

I always joked with him that he would spawn with anything that
twitched.   **Joan Fontaine**

DIANE ARBUS PHOTOGRAPHER

Giving a camera to Diane Arbus is like putting a live grenade in
the hands of a child.   **Norman Mailer**

JIM BAKKER FORMER TELEVISION EVANGELIST

I've been married to this man for twenty-six years and I can tell
you one thing: he's not homosexual, nor is he bisexual. He's a
wonderful, loving husband.   **Tammy Faye Bakker**

I have sat across the table from men who have told me of your
homosexual advances.   **Jerry Falwell**

CLIVE BARNES JOURNALIST, DANCE/DRAMA CRITIC

If I decide to stay around Broadway beyond the current season,
it will be for the pleasure of throwing his fat limey posterior out in
the street.   **David Merrick**

RONA BARRETT GOSSIP COLUMNIST

She doesn't need a steak knife. Rona cuts her food with her
tongue.   **Johnny Carson**

Congress should give a medal to her husband for waking up every
Sunday morning and looking at her.   **Frank Sinatra**

AUBREY BEARDSLEY ILLUSTRATOR

...a face like a silver hatchet, with grass-green hair.
                                                       Oscar Wilde

THOMAS HART BENTON PAINTER

He drove his kind of realism at me so hard I bounced right into
nonobjective painting.   **Jackson Pollock**

BILLY THE KID OLD WEST OUTLAW

Drank and laughed, rode and laughed, talked and laughed, fought and laughed, and killed and laughed.   **Pat Garrett**

JAMES BOND FICTIONAL BRITISH SPY

Bond is not my type at all. I like quiet, intelligent, sensitive men.
Barbara Bach (who is married to Ringo Starr)

I have always hated that damn James Bond. I'd like to kill him.
Sean Connery

He would be what I call the ideal defector. Because if the money was better, the booze freer and the women easier over there in Moscow, he'd be off like a shot. Bond, you see, is the ultimate prostitute.   **John Le Carré**

James Bond is a man of honor, a symbol of real value to the free world.   **Ronald Reagan**

He smoked like Peter Lorre and drank like Humphrey Bogart and ate like Sydney Greenstreet and used up girls like Errol Flynn and then went out to a steam bath and came out looking like Clark Gable.   **Harry Reasoner**

SANDRO BOTTICELLI PAINTER

If Botticelli were alive today, he'd be working for *Vogue*.
Peter Ustinov

RICHARD BRANSON
BRITISH ENTREPRENEUR, VIRGIN RECORDS/AIRLINES

Richard Branson's got ridiculously enormous teeth. One day all these cretins with big teeth and long hair and cheesecloth shirts started turning up at our gigs. These people were from Virgin Records.   **Andy Partridge**

BUDDHA PHILOSOPHER

Buddha was a good guy, but history is full of good guys.
Cliff Richard

JOEY BUTTAFUOCO   AUTO MECHANIC

I had a pretty good summer, kind of relaxing. I think I must have gone two months without saying the word "Buttafuoco."

David Letterman

He's the only person in the world more hated than I am.

Howard Stern

AL CAPONE   ORIGINAL SCARFACE

It was ironic that he, who was guilty of committing countless murders, had to be punished merely for failing to pay taxes on the money he had made by murder. **Herbert Hoover**

When the Emperor Constantine turned Christian, he banned the eating of sausage, which of course immediately created a whole army of sausage bootleggers and may explain why Al Capone always looked like a sausage. **Donald E. Westlake**

CINDY CRAWFORD   SUPERMODEL

When I heard Madonna was coming out with a nude photography book, I said, "Who wants to see Madonna nude?" If they did one on Cindy, *I'd* buy the book. **Francesco Scavullo**

SALVADOR DALI   ARTIST

Señor Dali, born delirious
Considers it folly to be serious. **Phyllis McGinley**

The two qualities that Dali unquestionably possesses are a gift for drawing and an atrocious egoism. **George Orwell**

He looks like something he painted. He has long, shiny black hair that keeps falling over his face, and he moves around like a cat full of gin. **H. Allen Smith**

The naked truth about me is to the naked truth about Salvador Dali as an old ukulele in the attic is to a piano in a tree, and I mean a piano with breasts. **James Thurber**

CHARLES DARWIN NATURALIST, EVOLUTIONIST

My theory of evolution is that Darwin was adopted.

Steven Wright

LEONARDO DA VINCI PAINTER, SCULPTOR, ARCHITECT, ENGINEER

He bores me. He ought to have stuck to his flying machines.

Auguste Renoir

SERGEY DIAGHILEV FOUNDER OF BALLET RUSSE

He could not bear the sight of Danilova and would say to me, "Her tits make me want to vomit."

George Balanchine

ISADORA DUNCAN DANCER

A woman whose face looked as if it had been made of sugar and someone had licked it.

George Bernard Shaw

ROGER EBERT FILM CRITIC

They released a big study about how bad movie-theater popcorn is for you. In fact, we went to the movies last night. The popcorn came in three sizes: Medium, large and "Roger Ebert's Tub of Death."

Jay Leno

MARY BAKER EDDY FOUNDER OF CHRISTIAN SCIENCE

The poor woman was obviously mentally adrift from the age of five, querulous, hysterical, unscrupulous, snobbish and almost unbelievably stupid....She had much in common with Hitler, only no moustache.

Noël Coward

...a brass god with clay legs.

Mark Twain

THOMAS EDISON INVENTOR

We owe a lot to Thomas Edison—if it wasn't for him, we'd be watching television by candlelight.

Milton Berle

ALBERT EINSTEIN PHYSICIST

If Mr. Einstein doesn't like the natural laws of the universe, let him go back to where he came from. **Robert Benchley**

What you're reaching for is never what you get. Einstein was mathematically trying to prove the existence of God. He winds up with the theory of relativity. **Dustin Hoffman**

The genius of Einstein leads to Hiroshima. **Pablo Picasso**

Even Albert Einstein reportedly needed help on his 1040 form. **Ronald Reagan**

Einstein explained his theory to me every day, and on my arrival I was fully convinced that he understood it. **Chaim Weizmann**

Einstein must have been like a gentle bright kitten trying to make friends with a child's balloon, very large and unaccountably unpuncturable. **H.G. Wells**

JACOB EPSTEIN SCULPTOR

I wish he would wash, but I believe Michelangelo *never* did, so I suppose it is part of the tradition. **Ezra Pound**

JERRY FALWELL EVANGELIST

Jerry Falwell says he's going to drive all those people out of office, magazines out of existence, books off library shelves. He's not only an Ayatollah, he's a Savonarola. He has a large hunting list. **James Michener**

BENJAMIN FRANKLIN
U.S. STATESMAN, PHILOSOPHER, SCIENTIST, INVENTOR, AUTHOR

Benjamin Franklin, incarnation of the peddling, tuppenny Yankee. **Jefferson Davis**

A philosophical Quaker full of mean and thrifty maxims. **John Keats**

Prudence is a wooden Juggernaut, before whom Benjamin Franklin walks with the portly air of a high priest. **Robert Louis Stevenson**

SIGMUND FREUD — FOUNDER OF PSYCHOANALYSIS

In my opinion, no self-respecting man ever paid the slightest attention to his dreams.
Cleveland Amory

Freud would have a heyday with me.
David Bowie

Sexuality evidently meant more to Freud than to other people.
Carl Jung

In my opinion he made a good job of dumping new loads on us and our consciences.
Henry Miller

I think he's crude, I think he's medieval, and I don't want an elderly gentleman from Vienna with an umbrella inflicting his dreams upon me.
Vladimir Nabokov

The greatest villain that ever lived, a man worse than Hitler or Stalin.
Telly Savalas

Sigmund Freud was a half-baked Viennese quack. Our literature, culture, and the films of Woody Allen would be better today if Freud had never written a word.
Ian Shoales

PAUL GAUGUIN — PAINTER

Don't talk to me of Gauguin. I'd like to wring the fellow's neck!
Paul Cézanne

ALBERTO GIACOMETTI — PAINTER

For him, to sculpt is to take the fat off space.
Jean-Paul Sartre

GOD — DEITY

How can I believe in God when just last week I got my tongue caught in the roller of an electric typewriter?
Woody Allen

I think there are innumerable gods. What we on earth call God is a little tribal God who has made an awful mess.
William S. Burroughs

The weak rely on Christ, the strong do not.
Richard Burton

Peter remained on friendly terms with Christ notwithstanding Christ's having healed his mother-in-law.
Samuel Butler

The devil tempted Christ, but it was Christ who tempted the devil to tempt him.   **Samuel Butler**

They say that God is everywhere, and yet we always think of Him as somewhat of a recluse.   **Emily Dickinson**

We're both Jewish, neither of us ever held a job, neither of us ever married, and we both traveled around the country irritating people.   **Kinky Friedman**

If God doesn't destroy Hollywood Boulevard, he owes Sodom and Gomorrah an apology.   **Jay Leno**

I just can't picture Jesus doing a whole lotta shakin'.
Jerry Lee Lewis

God must love the common man, he made so many of them.
Abraham Lincoln

"Sorry, Mickey," the Lord [will say], "but I wanted to give you the word personally. You can't go to heaven because of the way you acted down on earth, but would you mind signing a dozen baseballs?"   **Mickey Mantle**

God is a bore.   **H.L. Mencken**

God is a thought that makes crooked all that is straight.
Friedrich Nietzsche

I was raised Catholic and received the body and blood of Christ every Sunday at communion until the age of thirty, when I became a vegetarian.   **Joe Queenan**

God gave me my money.   **John D. Rockefeller**

I'm an atheist and I thank God for it.   **George Bernard Shaw**

A parish demagogue.   **Percy Bysshe Shelley**

I'm just not attracted to guys with beards. Maybe that's why Jesus bores me. Maybe if he shaved I'd dig him.   **Patti Smith**

When we talk to God, we're praying. When God talks to us, we're schizophrenic.   **Lily Tomlin**

One thing I have no worry about is whether God exists. But it has occurred to me that God has Alzheimer's and has forgotten we exist.   **Jane Wagner**

AL GOLDSTEIN PUBLISHER, *SCREW* MAGAZINE

He is a lovely man when he gets out of that sewer he operates
called *Screw*.   **Tom Snyder**

JOYCE HABER HOLLYWOOD GOSSIP

She needs open-heart surgery and they should go in through her
feet.   **Julie Andrews**

Joyce Haber of the *Los Angeles Times* once said that the difference between my audience and hers was that mine didn't read.
And she was right. They don't read her column, which often
duplicates much of my material.   **Rona Barrett**

JERRY HALL MODEL, ACTRESS

Try interviewing her sometime. It's like talking to a window.
                                                        Bryant Gumbel

PATTI HANSEN MODEL, ACTRESS

I love the bitch to death.   **Keith Richards**

HUGH HEFNER FOUNDER, *PLAYBOY* MAGAZINE

If he has done nothing else for American culture, he has given it
two of the great lies of the twentieth century: "I buy it for the fiction" and "I buy it for the interviews."   **Nora Ephron**

LEONA HELMSLEY HOTELIER, TAX FELON

The wicked witch of the west.   **Ed Koch**

She is a living nightmare, and to be married to her must be like
living in hell.   **Donald Trump**

MARGAUX HEMINGWAY MODEL, ACTRESS

A Hanukkah bush...the day after Christmas.
                                                        Mr. (Earl) Blackwell

CONRAD HILTON   HOTELIER

Conrad Hilton was very generous to me in the divorce settlement.
He gave me five thousand Gideon Bibles.   **Zsa Zsa Gabor**

HEDDA HOPPER   GOSSIP COLUMNIST

She was venomous, vicious, a pathological liar and quite stupid.
                                                        Ray Milland

Her virtue was that she said what she thought, her vice that what
she thought didn't amount to much.   **Peter Ustinov**

JACK THE RIPPER
19TH-CENTURY SERIAL KILLER, IDENTITY UNKNOWN

Cut quite a figure in his day.   **Groucho Marx**

BIANCA JAGGER   JET-SETTER

I like Bianca Jagger because she is one of the few women I know
who has as much class and style as I have.   **Britt Ekland**

I think she's got a lot of style but no breasts.   **Andy Warhol**

PAULINE KAEL   FILM CRITIC

Oh, fuck Pauline Kael, fuck her!...I don't care what she has to
say. She's a bitch. She's spiteful and she's wrong.

                                                    George Cukor

A demented bag lady.   **Alan Parker**

JOHN F. KENNEDY, JR.   ATTORNEY

It's pathetic. When I die, they are going to say, "Oh yeah, Sarah
once dated John Kennedy."   **Sarah Jessica Parker**

DOROTHY KILGALLEN   BROADWAY GOSSIP COLUMNIST

Dorothy Kilgallen is the only woman I wouldn't mind my wife
catching me with. I don't know why she took such umbrage at my
comments on birth control, she's such a living argument for it.
                                                    Johnny Carson

Having your taste criticized by Dorothy Kilgallen is like having your clothes criticized by Emmet Kelly. **Johnny Carson**

She must use Novocain lipstick. **Jack Paar**

CHARLES MANSON   MURDER MASTERMIND

You're a murderin' dog, Charlie. You're a mass-murderin' dog.
Geraldo Rivera

He would sit down with a guitar and start playing and making up stuff....Musically, I thought he was very unique. **Neil Young**

HENRI MATISSE   ARTIST

The goitrous, torpid and squinting husks provided by Matisse in his sculpture are worthless except as tactful decorations for a mental home. **Wyndham Lewis**

AIMEE SEMPLE McPHERSON   EVANGELIST

It may be that her autobiography is set down in sincerity, frankness and simple effort. It may be, too, that the Statue of Liberty is situated in Lake Ontario. **Dorothy Parker**

It is difficult to say whether Mrs. McPherson is happier in her crackling exclamations or in her bead-curtain-and-chenille-fringe style. Presumably the lady is happy in both manners. That would make her two up on me. **Dorothy Parker**

MARGARET MEAD   ANTHROPOLOGIST

Margaret Mead wasn't much help. What did I have in common with all those savages? **Erica Jong**

MICHELANGELO   PAINTER, SCULPTOR, ARCHITECT

If Michelangelo were a heterosexual, the Sistine Chapel would have been painted basic white and with a roller.
Rita Mae Brown

He was a good man but he did not know how to paint. **El Greco**

Michelangelo was a pornographer. **Camille Paglia**

CLAUDE MONET PAINTER

A skillful but short-lived decorator.   **Edgar Degas**

WILLIAM MORRIS ARTIST, ARCHITECT, AUTHOR

Of course we all know that Morris was a wonderful all-round man, but the act of walking round him has always tired me.

Max Beerbohm

MUHAMMAD FOUNDER OF ISLAM

The kingdom of Muhammad is a kingdom of revenge, of wrath and desolation.   **Martin Luther**

ISAAC NEWTON PHYSICIST, MATHEMATICIAN

Newton *was* a great man, but you must excuse me if I think that it would take many Newtons to make one Milton.

Samuel Taylor Coleridge

...was so absorbed in his pursuits as to be something of a changeling in worldly matters; and when he descended to earth and conjecture he was no phenomenon.   **Horace Walpole**

RUDOLF NUREYEV BALLET DANCER

Someone...said he thought Richard Nixon was obviously homosexual. I said, "Why do you think that?" He said, "You know, that funny uncoordinated way he moves." I said, "Yeah—like Nureyev."   **Gore Vidal**

WILLIAM PALEY THEOLOGIAN, PHILOSOPHER

He looks like a man who has just swallowed an entire human being.   **Truman Capote**

LOUELLA PARSONS GOSSIP COLUMNIST

Louella is stronger than Samson. He needed two columns to bring the house down. Louella can do it with one.   **Samuel Goldwyn**

In her own field, where bad writing is as natural and as common as breathing, Louella's stands out like an asthmatic's gasps.

Nunnally Johnson

Not a bad old slob. **James Mason**

Louella looked like a very old tadpole. **Lilli Palmer**

Her sneakiest and most valuable asset was looking either stupid or drunk and getting exclusives in the process. **Robert Stack**

NORMAN VINCENT PEALE CLERGYMAN, AUTHOR

I find Paul appealing but Peale appalling. **Adlai Stevenson**

WESTBROOK PEGLER JOURNALIST

The Presstitute. **Walter Winchell**

PABLO PICASSO ARTIST

Picasso kept finding new ways of avoiding maturity.

Clive James

My little granddaughter of six could do as well.

Norman Rockwell

JACKSON POLLOCK PAINTER

I can't see the point of those drips and I think he couldn't do anything else particularly well. **Francis Bacon**

REX REED FILM CRITIC, AUTHOR

When Rex Reed wrote that I had a face like an open sandwich, that was the best moment so far. It's just a thing of mine—I've always wanted to be compared to deli food. **Albert Brooks**

Rex Reed is either at your feet or at your throat. **Ava Gardner**

Reed is a frustrated little man who wanted to become an actor but couldn't make it. **Otto Preminger**

You wouldn't believe some of the things they've said about me. Like Rex Reed saying my career is more mysterious than cot death!
Sylvester Stallone

If I had an affair with Jack the Ripper, the offspring would be Rex Reed.
Jacqueline Susann

ORAL ROBERTS — EVANGELIST

I never thought God would hold someone accountable for not raising money.
Pat Robertson

WILL ROGERS — ACTOR, "COWBOY PHILOSOPHER"

The bosom friend of senators and congressmen was about as daring as an early Shirley Temple movie.
James Thurber

YVES SAINT-LAURENT — FASHION DESIGNER

Saint-Laurent has excellent taste. The more he copies me, the better taste he displays.
Coco Chanel

JOHN SINGER SARGENT — PAINTER

A sepulchre of dulness [*sic*] and propriety.
James McNeill Whistler

JOHN SIMON — DRAMA/FILM CRITIC, WRITER

. . .a man whose brain is being demented by the bile rising from his bowels. I don't want to be reviewed by Dracula.
Norman Mailer

Frank Rich and John Simon are the syphilis and gonorrhea of the theater.
David Mamet

What a nightmare, to wake up in the morning and realize that you are John Simon.
Gore Vidal

ELIZABETH CADY STANTON — SUFFRAGIST

As usual, when she had fired her gun she went home and left me to finish the battle.
Susan B. Anthony

TINTORETTO PAINTER

He will never be anything but a dauber.

Titian

DONALD TRUMP BUSINESS ENTREPRENEUR

Marla Maples says she won't need a prenuptial agreement if she marries Donald Trump because "our relationship is built on trust." And she's right...if you can't trust the married man you've been running around with, who can you trust?

Johnny Carson

Piggy, piggy, piggy.

Ed Koch

Prior to the Reagan era, the newly rich aped the old rich. But that isn't true any longer. Donald Trump is making no effort to behave like Eleanor Roosevelt as far as I can see.

Fran Lebowitz

He is very down to earth in his demands, and in his lifestyle he's quite simple.

Ivana Trump

IVANA TRUMP SOCIALITE, WRITER

I think she dresses much too flashy. I also think her hair is ridiculous, and I think her behavior with Donald was very stupid. All she cares about is money, money, money. I hate that.

Zsa Zsa Gabor

Ivana and I are friends, but we're very different. She married a rich man. I earned everything I have.

Eva Gabor

KENNETH TYNAN DRAMA/FILM CRITIC

...carried on the great and lucrative English tradition of charging the United States a handsome sum of money for telling us how ugly we are.

William F. Buckley, Jr.

GLORIA VANDERBILT DESIGNING WOMAN

She's taken her good family name and put it on the asses of America!

Gilda Radner

Frankly, I wouldn't want Gloria's name on my tail and I'm surprised she'd want it there either.

Andy Rooney

VINCENT VAN GOGH PAINTER

When people said I might be drinking too much I would say, "Van Gogh said he had to drink for a whole summer to find that yellow." But he was probably so drunk he couldn't find the tube.

Dennis Hopper

DIANA VREELAND FASHION MAGAZINE EDITOR

She is pure *Alice in Wonderland* and her appearance and demeanor are a nicely judged mix of the Red Queen and a flamingo.

Truman Capote

ANDY WARHOL ARTIST, FILMMAKER

He's a sphinx without a secret.

Truman Capote

He's an idiot, like a big cheesecake on legs.

Boy George

Andy Warhol was a very lucky man. He couldn't paint, couldn't dress, couldn't talk. Even so, he became famous and obscenely rich. Who says that talent pays?

Paulette Goddard

He was absolutely crazy about collecting images. He would take millions of pictures—which is very *annoying* when you're eating your soup and you've just blurped a piece of minestrone down your chin.

Mick Jagger

Although one of his long-standing fantasies was to open a house of prostitution, the fantasy role he chose for himself was that of cashier.

Jesse Kornbluth

He is the only genius with an IQ of 60.

Gore Vidal

JAMES McNEILL WHISTLER PAINTER

Whistler once made London a half-way house between New York and Paris and wrote rude things in the visitors' book.

Max Beerbohm

I have seen and heard much of Cockney impudence before now; but never expected to hear a coxcomb ask two hundred guineas for flinging a pot of paint in the public's face.   **John Ruskin**

As for borrowing Mr. Whistler's ideas about art, the only thoroughly original ideas I have ever heard him express have had reference to his own superiority as a painter over painters greater than himself.   **Oscar Wilde**

A miniature Mephistopheles, mocking the majority. **Oscar Wilde**

EARL WILSON GOSSIPMONGER

He has a strange growth on his neck—his head.   **Arthur Godfrey**

WALTER WINCHELL NEW YORK GOSSIP COLUMNIST

I don't see why Walter Winchell is allowed to live.

Ethel Barrymore

Has anyone ever criticized you for bleating over the radio week- and two-week-old news and yelping "Scoop!" or "Exclusive!"?

W.C. Fields

Poor Walter. He's afraid he'll wake up some day and discover he's not Walter Winchell.   **Dorothy Parker**

...[a] gent's room journalist.   **Westbrook Pegler**

BRIGHAM YOUNG MORMON LEADER

He is dreadfully married. He's the most married man I ever saw in my life.   **Artemus Ward**

Index

(Note: Boldfaced names and page numbers indicate the subjects of the quotes and where they are featured.)